THE PROJECT MANAGER ADVENTURES

Pierre Kouhozon

ISBN: 9781791888602

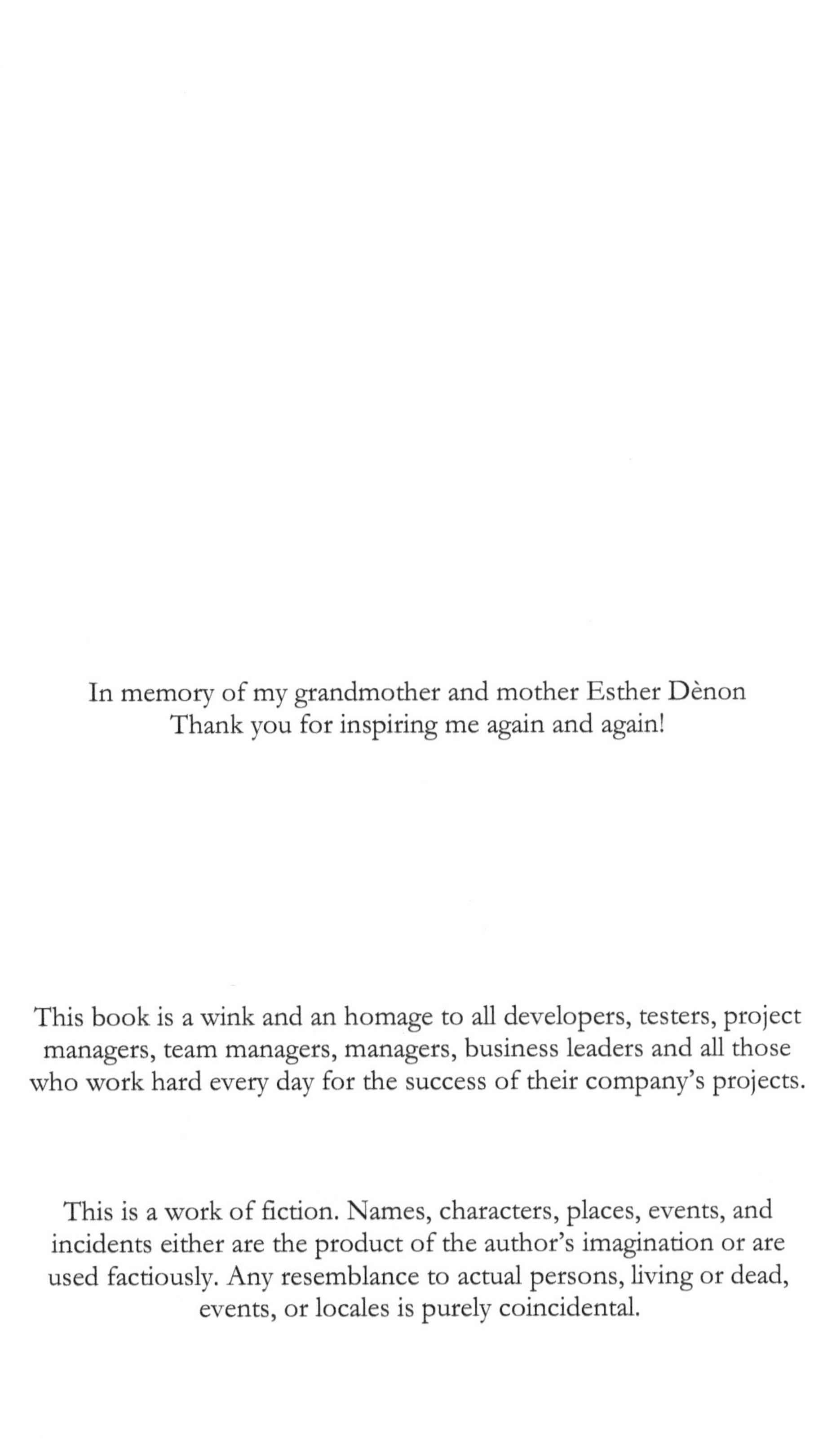

In memory of my grandmother and mother Esther Dènon
Thank you for inspiring me again and again!

This book is a wink and an homage to all developers, testers, project managers, team managers, managers, business leaders and all those who work hard every day for the success of their company's projects.

This is a work of fiction. Names, characters, places, events, and incidents either are the product of the author's imagination or are used factiously. Any resemblance to actual persons, living or dead, events, or locales is purely coincidental.

CONTENTS

Section 1: The scenario…

PROLOGUE

AssurTGE is a company specializing in the insurance of very large companies.

It has established itself in European countries through twenty-seven subsidiaries. Christophe Proudy, 55 years old, graying hair, is the current CEO (Chief Executive Officer). Each subsidiary develops and runs its agencies' network. In France, the network has fifty agencies. To expand its activities, the multinational insurance Globalinrance acquires it in August 2020.

Historically, each subsidiary uses its local management software in its network. The softwares are interfaced with other tools in accounting, corporate finance, market finance, procurement, and logistics. Some modules of market finance and logistics are accessible from mobile terminals.

As part of a program designed to standardize the group's information system, AssurTGE launches the project "AlphaProject" that will provide a new centralized management software called "Centragiciel". This software will help to manage the flow of information between all affiliates.

The project started two years ago. The deadlines were communicated to all subsidiaries. But the implementation is not going as planned: the schedule of the intermediate deliveries slip endlessly, the budget is not under control anymore, the quality of the deliveries is below expectations, the team's morale is affected, the directors of the subsidiaries have lost hope and no longer believe in the success of the project. Christophe Proudy then hires a professional project manager to get the project back on track.

It is spring. In the early afternoon, the president of Globalinrance, accompanied by his team, arrives unexpectedly on the new AssurTGE's European site in Brussels. Christophe gives them a tour of the premises.

The building, modern and oval-shaped, has ten floors and several entrances. In its vast courtyard, there are several squares of colorful gardens, water fountains and rows of shrubs rigorously aligned. Taking advantage of the first rays of sunshine, groups of employees sit on the lawn, holding meetings with their laptops placed on their knees for some, or their notebook in their hands for others.

Its four large buildings called "North-West", "North-East", "South-West" and "South-East" are connected by some long and spacious walkways. Each building has its own canteens, several video conferencing rooms, resting areas, private chat rooms, babysitting, nurseries, swimming pools, gymnasiums and many nap cabins.

Christophe starts the visit in his own office which is located on the top floor of the "South-East" building. Then, he leads the group to the "Business Department" whose offices are spread over several floors. The director, a tall brunette with short hair of about fifty years old, shows them the "Finance-Accounting" office, the "Marketing-Sales" office, the "Customer Relationship" office, the "Human Resources" office, the "Communication" office and the "Legal Affairs" office.

They head to the "North-West" building, which contains a part of the "Information Systems Department" (ISD), and visit two of its main offices: "Operations & Production" and "Maintenance & Support".

They go down to the fifth floor where some research and development (R & D) teams are located. Suddenly, the President of Globalinrance stops, contemplative: the whole floor is a large platform divided into several squares separated by long corridors, like New York streets. Panels and arrows indicate directions to facilitate orientation. Most of the employees are standing in the squares; very few people are seated. Christophe explains to the group that the desks are adjustable in height to work in a "standing" or "sitting" position and many choose to remain standing most of the time to force themselves to move more often. "Impressive!" exclaims someone of the group and they head to the "Quality Department" office.

To end the visit, the President of Globalinrance thanks Christophe and his team for the work they are doing and reiterates that he is counting on them to achieve AssurTGE objectives as soon as possible. He recalls that the stakes are high and asks his deputy to follow the project personally.

Figure 1-1 shows the AssurTGE organization chart.

Figure 1-1. AssurTGE organization chart

1

It’s 8 am. AssurTGE employees begin arriving at the office. Many drop off their stuff and head to the cafeteria for breakfast. Alfan and Ethan, two developers whose offices are opposite each other, turn on their computers as soon as they arrive. Alfan connects to a news website while Ethan displays on his screen the defect report on which he had worked the day before.

Suddenly, Alfan raises his head and looks towards Ethan.

“Ethan, did you get Christophe's email? He has just sent it. Well, look at your emails, it seems he’s got a surprise for us.”

“Oh ... no ... What else does he want?” Ethan says.

He opens his mailbox and reads Christophe's email: “Thanks to all the ISD teams to meet in conference hall B at 12 o'clock”.

“Couldn’t he choose 2 pm? Isn’t 12’ oclock lunchtime?”

“I have a conference call with Italy’s customer care manager at noon. It’s very difficult to find an available time slot with him. Anyway, I'll have to postpone it.”

Alfan gets up and heads towards the cafeteria, murmuring, “Okay, but it's not by canceling meetings that we’ll make progress on our works...”

It's noon. All ISD teams go to the large conference hall on the ground floor. The hall is completely filled. They are standing and waiting for Christophe. He arrives, approaches the microphone and begins:

"Hello everyone."

Total silence. Suddenly, a shrill noise! An alarm starts ringing. The hubbub of the crowd accompanies the deafening sound of the alarm. Security guards arrive and direct the crowd to outside, away from the building. Small groups are formed.

"Is there a fire?" an employee in the crowd yells.

"Nobody knows, but you have to get away in any case, it's security!" another one further replies.

Other groups comment on Christophe's email. Some wondered what was going on; others, how could what he was going to tell them be so urgent. Many assumed that he wanted to announce the arrival of a new vice president, as the rumors that had been circulating for a few days was suggesting.

About thirty minutes later, the security guards order them to return. The crowd progressively goes back to the building. The conference hall fills up again. Christophe approaches the microphone and begins.

"First of all, I'm sorry to disturb your plans. I'll be brief. I'm informing you that our CIO, Clauspel Roan, resigned this morning. From the minutes that follow, while waiting for a final replacement, Tom Troyas will own all his activities. Do you have any questions?"

Tom, a man of about forty years old, tall and athletic, kind of ruddy-faced, has been working for several years with Christophe. He strokes his thick mustache softly to welcome the news. An employee of the crowd shouts from afar to be heard:

"Could you please tell us the reasons for that sudden departure?"

"As you know, our number one priority is the success of the Information Systems merge I initiated two years ago. I know you have been working hard on that. But, so far, this program is still at a standstill and is not moving forward as it should. Worse, subsidiaries managers complain every day about the way things are going on. I want it back on track immediately, and this requires hard decisions. Another question?"

"Yes, I have one!" a man from the crowd cries out.

Everyone turns the head to try to see who is going to speak.

"Well, what is then your action plan to get the project back on track?"

Tom Troyas immediately approaches the microphone and speaks.

"I'm not going to detail everything here. Our consulting firm is going to send us a new project manager to replace Clement who has done what he could so far: His name is Alan Sapin. Some of you told me that they have had the chance to work with him; he has a great experience in major projects and is certified in the methodologies for managing large projects. He will take over the project starting from tomorrow morning."

"Another question?" Christophe asks.

"I don't want to be a preacher," an employee from the back of the hall says. "But how can you expect an external person, as experienced and certified as he is, to be able to recover such a situation? I'd like to see how he's going to do, that guy!"

"OK, I see that there're no more questions. So, enjoy your lunch" Christophe concludes.

Teams return to their offices in groups, some go to canteen. Everyone comments on Clauspel's departure in his own way.

8:30 am the next morning. A man in his mid-40s, dressed in a dark suit, a light blue shirt and a dark blue tie, arrives at AssurTGE's reception desk. He wears square glasses that hide his blue eyes, walks firmly and looks sympathetic: it is Alan. One of the receptionists accompanies him to Tom Troyas office. The desk is very large and tidy. Above, there is a large framed picture of his family. In the photo, there is next to Tom, a blonde woman smiling. Two little girls and a boy of about ten years surround them. The girls look eight and five years old.

"Hello Tom, Alan Sapin!" Alan says, holding out his hand while looking straight in Tom's eye.

"Welcome, Alan!" Tom replies as he gets up to shake his hand. "Put your stuff in my office and follow me. Let's go to the cafeteria to start the day off right."

They go into the elevator. Tom keeps talking.

"Well, the task will be tough, but I think you're used to it. You have to be careful with the interaction; it is very sensitive here; you won't have many friends. As soon as we go up, I will introduce you to the different teams and then you will settle down. We will have lunch together at one pm and catch up later at the end of the day. Is this okay for you?

"Perfect!" Alan replies.

They arrive at the cafeteria. Alan orders a coffee and a croissant. Tom chooses a chocolate bread and a hot chocolate drink. They comment on political scandals constantly revealed in the media, the frequent incidents on the subway lines, and many other trivial subjects. After breakfast, they take the elevator and go upstairs.

"Here is the workspace of a part of the R & D; the Marketing teams are in another building," Tom explains.

"OK, are we going to see them after?"

"Yeah! Look! top management has invested much money in this project. All these people have been working hard from the beginning."

"I see."

"But the project is not making any progress despite all these efforts. It's frustrating!"

"Yeah, I imagine, it would be."

On the either side of the corridor, there is a large space, full of offices, that is being filled progressively. Employees meet, greet each other and settle. Tom encounters a colleague and stops.

"Hi Franck, this is Alan Sapin, our new project manager."

"Ah ... is it the next one who is going to be used as a scapegoat?" Franck replies, jokingly.

"Stop it! It's true that his task won't be easy. How to sort all this mess out?"

"Good luck, Alan!"

"Thanks. So, tell me, Franck, what do you do?" Alan asks.

Tom responds quickly, "Franck is the manager of the maintenance and support team."

"Yes, that's it," Franck adds. "My team has to face all the incidents that users raise when the project team releases into production a low-quality product."

It's 9:30 am. The teams are almost all in their offices. Tom introduces Alan to the main people of ISD with whom he will have to work: analysts, architects, integrators, quality teams, maintenance, and production. They continue going around the offices.

"So, let's go and see the business managers."

They walk along a corridor and head to the "South-East" building. Tom calls the elevator and they go to the marketing department offices.

"Hi Flavienne, this is Alan, the new AlphaProject project manager", Tom says.

"Good morning Flavienne", Alan adds.

Flavienne stands and offers his hand in greeting Alan, smiling.

"Hello Alan, welcome! Are you our savior? Are we going to be delivered on time then? Will the schedule stop slipping? R & D keeps postponing, there's always a problem. And for our products in production, there's no day without critical incidents. We have users on the back every day, that's unbearable. Do you see what I mean? You have a heavy responsibility."

"We'll try to sort all this out, I'll see you again if you have a bit of time. See you later, then!"

2

Tom introduces Alan to the other business departments. As he approached his office, he stops, turns to Alan and says:

"By the way, I'm not sure all the business needs have been considered. I've heard some people grumble in the cafeteria. They were complaining that no one has involved them so far on the project. But, we can't work on everything either, given the very short deadlines. That is business team problem; it's up to them to agree with each other!"

"OK, I'll take that into account," Alan says.

"But, precisely, how are you going to manage all this mess?" Tom asks dubiously.

"I'll get the picture of the situation, question the people who are working on the project and identify what worked and what did not work. Then, it should be clearer in my mind."

They move again and walk more quickly.

"Question people? Okay, but do not spend too much time on that. Management has already set the deadlines and we have committed. So, do not consume too much team's time on that. Well, even better, I can answer the questions in their place, it will save them time."

"I understand. It will still be useful for me to meet each person, at least the main people."

"That will take time. You'll see, they won't have enough time to dedicate to that and mostly won't be able to free themselves quickly."

"OK, if you give me a list of the main people who have an interest in the project, I'll manage to meet them soon."

Tom accompanies Alan to where he will sit and heads to a meeting room. Alan office is located on two-floor levels below Tom's.

In the middle of the afternoon, Alan calls him.

"Tom, tell me, is there a 'Project Charter' in the project repository?"

"What do you mean by Project Charter?"

"Uh ... Let's say a document that Christophe would have communicated to the teams to formally authorize the project and give authority to the project manager to allocate AssurTGE's resources to AlphaProject's activities. In general, it also contains the initial requirements that meet the needs and stakeholder expectations."

"Stakeholder! Do you mean those who are working on the project?"

"Yes, and any other person or organization that AlphaProject can impact positively or negatively, upon" Alan responds. "They may have an influence on the project, but not necessarily at the same level. I have to analyze all that to better manage them."

"Hmm, I'm sending you a document that looks like it. It's the one we used to present the project, some slides contain these elements you mention. However, I don't think we should waste time on these documents, we aren't going to restart the project from the beginning! We are rather expected firmly to meet the next deadlines."

"I understand, send it to me. Thank you."

Alan looks forward to opening the document as soon as he receives Tom's email. It's a description of the stakes and objectives of the project, how it is structured, and the major deadlines set by Christophe. A second document is attached to the mail. He opens it: it's the list of people he can contact for the interview. He thinks for a moment, grabs his desk phone and calls the first person on the list.

"Hello, Flavienne! Do you have a minute?"

"Yes, what is it about?"

"I'd like to interview some of the people who have worked on AlphaProject so far. Obviously, you are one of those who can enlighten me."

"OK, but not this week. And next week, I won't be in the office. This brings us to two weeks. Is this okay?"

"You really can't before? It won't take us more than an hour."

"All topics are urgent in this company. Sorry, but I don't see how it could be sooner. Tom has also followed the project in every detail, he can answer all your questions, I think, and that will save us time."

"Yeah, but it will also be better if I can meet you."

"OK. Anyway, I note that we will meet in two weeks, Monday the 23rd from 11 am to noon. I'll send you the confirmation."

"Thanks, Flavienne."

"By the way, do not forget, the upcoming deadlines are eagerly awaited!" Flavienne recalls just before hanging up.

Alan hangs up as well. A few minutes later, he goes to see Franck, the manager of maintenance and support.

"Hello Franck, I'd like to meet you for an hour during the week for an interview on AlphaProject. Is this possible?"

"I'm very busy. Can we do that next week?"

Franck opens his electronic organizer and starts speaking to himself while browsing it: “no room, no room, no room”. He turns to Alan and continues.

“Anyway, no one asked me what my expectations on this project were. So, I’m not sure I can really help you.”

“I see. It's never too late to do well. So, suggest a slot and you'll see that you'll be useful to me.”

“Friday, next week!”

Alan contacts all department managers. None of them is available in the week. Subsidiaries managers are also all busy. He returns to his office. Sitting in his seat, he turns his back on his computer, closes his eyes and focuses. Thoughts start passing through his mind: *Total absence of project manager's authority, no formal definition of roles ... Alan, you must act right now to unblock the situation! You are now responsible for this project. Ask the sponsor for his official support. Write the Project Charter very quickly and have it validated by Christophe, he is the sponsor. This should lead you to the Project Management Plan that doesn’t even exist on this project! Come on, hang in there, Alan! Act immediately!* Suddenly he opens his eyes, picks up his phone and calls Tom.

“Tom, I have to write a project charter based on the information you know and have it validated by Christophe. It will further clarify the roles, the project objectives and above all, will give authority to the project manager. Do you have any template of this kind of document? Or an example from a past project?”

“Template? No! At the beginning of the projects, we write some documents to communicate about the project. This is the document I sent you. There’s no particular template, everyone does as he wants.”

Silence for a few moments.

“You can search on the extranet,” Tom continues. “Some templates of project documents are stored there. You may find an equivalent of your famous Project Charter. But frankly, we are not very 'project documents' here. It's time-consuming and looks like administrative paperwork!"

"OK, I have the slides. The business opportunity document and your explanations should be sufficient to start with."

Alan books a time slot with Tom and asks him questions about the additional information he needs. Tom gives details on the project justification, its objectives as well as the requirements. To gather details about the stakeholders, Alan displays a table named "StakeholderRegister" structured as below:

Name	Title	Site	Contact Information	Role in Project	Expectations	Interest	Influence	Classification
C.Proudy	President	BE	-	Sponsor	Subsidiaries Satisfaction	High	High	Support

Table 1-1. Stakeholder register structure

Together, they fill it with the main stakeholders' information and obtain the list, the extract of which is seen in the Appendix 2. They discuss the options of some key resources assignment and decide to finalize the discussion with Christophe. Alan proposes the list of deliverables that will be approved by Christophe or by people he would delegate to do so and suggests a list of the risks he can see on the project.

He returns to his office and writes a document that is two pages long and specifies the points below (see Appendix 1):

- ✓ Project Title and Short Description
- ✓ Project justification
- ✓ Measurable objectives of the project
- ✓ Project Manager and Authority Level
- ✓ Assigned resources
- ✓ Stakeholders
- ✓ Requirements of known stakeholders
- ✓ Product Description / Deliverables
- ✓ Project acceptance requirements
- ✓ High-level risks of the project
- ✓ Project sponsor

He makes some changes that Tom asks, meets with Christophe and explains why he wants him to validate the document and publish it himself. Christophe completes the list of resources assigned, hesitates a little on the deliverables that he will have to approve, validates the document, then distributes it to all AssurTGE departments and the subsidiaries directors.

Immediately, the situation is unblocked, the department heads call Alan and offer him slots in the week for interviews. He is happy to have finally the attention of the main people involved in the project.

His phone rings. Tom.

"You were right Alan, now the goals are even clearer to me, and we know who should do what at this stage of the project. Formalize enlightens, I knew that well!"

"Exactly!"

"You talked a lot about interviews, but, how will they allow you to move forward?" Tom asks.

"It'll be a surprise," Alan replies with a smile. "I won't tell you everything, right now!"

3

Alan is about to start the interviews. He goes to the Marketing-Sales manager office.

"Hello, Diane!"

"Hi, Alan. Come in."

Diane goes to a small coffee machine next to her desk and makes herself a coffee. Alan puts his laptop on the desk, turns it on, and displays the list of questions he has prepared.

"Alan, would you like a coffee? Or tea?" Diane asks from afar.

"No thanks, I've just had one."

Diane takes her cup and walks towards Alan. Even before sitting down, she asks:

"So, how can I help you?"

"The purpose of this interview is to gather as much information as possible about the major events that occur on the project. More importantly, it's an opportunity to have a very first contact with you and know your expectations and interests. All these elements will help me to reorganize the project by learning from what went wrong so far and take advantage of what went well."

"OK, good approach!"

"Yeah, and do not hesitate to tell me clearly, according to you, what went wrong, or ... well."

"Uh… 'Went well'? That will be quick!"

Diane takes a sip of her coffee and resumes.

"I am the head of the Marketing-Sales department. You know, in addition to our core business, we provide business consulting services. I develop this activity as well. With my team, we are in charge of six subsidiaries: France, Spain, Germany, Ireland, Italy and Finland. The twenty-one others are spread among my other colleagues."

"Fine!"

"We worked with R & D on our needs and expectations. They are familiar with our current tools. We asked for the merge to be transparent to us. Subsidiaries have many specificities that are essential for users and they must find them in the new version."

After each answer, Alan pauses for a few seconds before moving on to the next question.

"OK, I understand that there are not so many problems at your level about the expected functionalities. Regarding the organization and the progress of the project, in your view, what are the events that went wrong? or went well?"

"Well, at a moment, we use to meet regularly in meetings; we were really one team, which was fine. But it was at the beginning! However, R & D didn't meet its commitments, and that's the big problem!"

Diane takes a deep breath, gets up, puts down her empty coffee mug next to the machine, put her hands into the pockets, returns to her desk and continues without sitting down.

"Delivery date postponements disrupt business activities seriously and cause us to lose revenue. You know, we needed this new tool for yesterday! But, they postponed the first module delivery date several times. And when they deliver, the module is simply useless and does not pass the quality tests or it misses half of the main expected functions. Anyway, it's like starting all over again after each delivery."

"OK, I'm here to get the project back on track. If everyone works in the same direction, we'll get there. What do you think are some risks for the project? or success factors?

"At the very beginning of the project, I listed in a document a number of risks and key success factors. They are still relevant. No one has done anything to at least reduce the risks and exploit the success factors."

Diane turns on her laptop, does a quick search and waits a few seconds.

"Yes, here it is! Let me send it to you by email right away!" she says, happy to have found the document she is looking for.

"From your point of view, what benefits will AlphaProject bring you?"

"It's clear that the final product will increase the productivity of my department and therefore that of the whole company. For example, currently, many treatments are still done manually. It's very complicated to collect information and consolidate them. In the end, we come up with unreliable output after much effort. We are all looking forward to this tool."

"You have a strong expectation and interest in this project. That's right?"

"Exactly!"

Diane's phone rings. She looks at the number, smiles and speaks to Alan.

"It's Christophe, I have to answer."

She picks up the phone and starts talking, staring at a picture on the wall.

"Yes, Christophe ... OK ... you like the report then ... Perfect ... Tomorrow six thirty pm in your office ... OK".

She hangs up and turns to Alan after having recovered her spirits, as very happy with her

conversation.

"It looks like you're close to Christophe!" Alan says, smiling.

"Yes, he likes to listen to my recommendations. In fact, he listens to all his close collaborators. He is a good boss! He often says that I have influence over the directors of the subsidiaries I'm in charge of. In general, the other directors follow them when they have to make a decision together."

"It's interesting to know, for the communication strategy on the project!" comments Alan. "So, coming back to our interview, how are you going to measure the success of the project? What will make you say that the project is successful or a failure?"

"Oh ... that's very simple! It's sufficient that the merge ends quickly as we were promised and the subsidiaries are satisfied with the use of the new tools."

"Thanks for your contribution, Diane. How often do you want to be informed about the progress of the project?"

"I liked the report of the progress your predecessor used to send every week."

"Are there other topics you'd like to discuss that we haven't talked about?"

"No, I think we've gone around. Count on me, I will contact you if I have anything else to discuss."

Flavienne is the manager of Customer Relationship department. Her office is close to Diane's one. Alan goes there and starts the interview. He presents the purpose of the interview, refers to the questions he has prepared and asks his first question to which Flavienne responds:

"My department manages the relationship with the subsidiaries and assists them in solving the administrative problems they meet. There are many complaints."

"OK"

"With my team, we're in charge of Poland, Romania, Slovakia, Slovenia, Hungary, and the Czech Republic."

"So, East!" Alan remarks.

"Yes! We have specified most of our needs. But there are still some functional modules that are not yet mastered. At least, we specified all that in a document. R & D guys put pressure on us saying they can't move forward until they receive full specifications."

"And how do you manage that?"

"We deliver all modules including parts that are still unclear. And in return, they blame us when they deliver, in test environment, unusable applications."

"Really?"

Alan continues with the same questions he asked Diane. Flavienne also relies on AlphaProject to reduce her team workload. She thinks that specifications deadline is often short, as specifying is new to her teams.

At the end of the interview, Alan meets Tom in his office. They sit at a round table at the right corner of the entrance.

"Let me explain to you how the implementation team is organized," Tom says. "There are the development team and the test team. Part of the development team is divided into seven groups of seven developers. A senior developer leads each group. He is the technical lead. And we have seven distributions of this type!"

"Oh yes, that's a lot of people."

"Yes! But for the moment, I'm going to talk to you about only the groups you'll be dealing with right away. To distinguish them easily, we named them with Greek alphabet letters. Thus, there are Alpha, Beta, Gamma, Delta, Epsilon, Zeta, and Eta groups."

"Great! Do you include the group leader among the seven developers?"

"Yes! He's part of it. Alfan is in charge of the group Alpha, Betty the group Beta, Gama the group Gamma, Delly the group Delta, Esin the group Epsilon, Zely for the group Zeta and Ethan the group Eta."

"Not hard to remember! Did you choose the group leaders based on their first name? Alan asks with a smile. You said earlier that teams are developing a part of the accounting module".

"You'll know all the modules better over time. But, yes, we started with this part because it could be released quickly to users into production independently of the other parts."

"Good!"

"The duration of implementation is initially estimated at six months. Well, I mean its development, validation and deployment. It's been a year now since they started working on it. And believe me, it's only a tenth of the job!"

"A year?"

"Yes, a year! We keep postponing the rollout date."

"And you have already announced a new date?"

"Yes! The last was announced by Christophe himself. And it's in a month! When he announced your arrival, he communicated as well that new deadline to all AssurTGE."

"So, in a month, we'll have to release something into production. And what is the current status?"

"Well, I will let you discover that! But I heard this morning that we're very far from being able to meet this deadline. And this worries me a lot!"

Tom takes a deep breath.

"All I can tell you," he continues, "is that right now, the quality team is testing one part, and the developers are developing another which is supposed to be delivered in a week in tests. And the news is not good at all!"

"Not good at all. What do you mean?" Alan asks.

"You should liaise with these two teams as soon as possible to see where the blockage is. Under no circumstances can we afford to delay the delivery. Otherwise, we'll simply be fired!"

"My first weekly meeting with managers is scheduled for tomorrow; I'll have a chance to know more then."

Tom glances at her watch.

"I have another meeting in a quarter of an hour," he says. "I have to get ready. I think we've gone around the situation."

"OK, I also think so."

4

Alan completes the synthesis of the interviews he has already done and goes to the R & D department head, Chris'office. He explains to him the purpose of the interview and lets him start speaking.

"All the work is done in my department," Chris begins. "The technical teams work for me. I mean integrators, developers and architects. All of them are involved in our projects."

"OK"

"I followed this project closely. Business teams hardly agree on their needs. They deliver incomplete specifications and often late. But they expect in return their product to be bug-free. And especially, they're never available to answer developer questions when needed."

"Hum, how would you explain the repeated schedule slippage?"

It's very simple! Devs teams receive some modules specifications very late. On top of that, there are many change requests when developments are already too advanced. Some subsidiaries wake up at the last moment and their requests flow; and the initial deadline must remain the same and can't be extended, of course!"

"So, how did the project manager handle that?"

"Well ... the schedule slips, that's all. And they blame my teams. I have the list of all those late change requests."

"OK, no problem with the lack of resource?"

Chris gets up, walks around the office, grabs the anti-stress next to his computer and starts playing with it while responding.

"Ah ... I was keeping that one for the end. It's just painful! It's very difficult to dedicate resources to a project here. To give you an idea, more than half of the developers who work on AlphaProject also intervene for at least five days a month on other activities to help with urgent problems. And this is the case for all our projects."

Chris leans forward towards Alan and continues by lowering his voice slightly.

"I let you imagine the impacts!"

"What are you expecting from AlphaProject now?"

"This is our first experience of such a large project. I would like it to serve us as a lesson learned and… we capitalize on best practices to succeed with our upcoming projects. If at the end, all AssurTGE teams understand how important it is to work together as a team in the same direction, we'll have won."

"That's for sure!" Alan confirms.

"One last thing Alan! I'm afraid that we've seriously underestimated the project. And therefore, resources allocated are not up to the objectives."

Alan finishes the interview and takes a look at his watch. 6:30 pm. It's time to review the day's activities. He rushes to Tom's office and finds his door closed. He returns to his office, his phone flashing alerting him that there are new messages. He picks up the handset and presses the voicemail key. Tom's voice: *"Alan, I was called urgently into Christophe's office, let's postpone our review to tomorrow at the same time. See you tomorrow then!"*

Yu, the test team manager, is walking down the hall, looking tired, undoubtedly exhausted after a hard and long day's work. He is walking fast as if he's in a hurry to get out of the building. He sees Alan and says from afar:

"Hello Alan, we'll see each other tomorrow morning nine thirty. Correct?"

"That's correct, Yu! Have a good evening."

Alan reviews the interviews he has done in the day, summarizes them in a file and saves it in the project's repository. It's 7:30 pm. His mobile phone rings. Without checking the caller number, he smiles and replies, "Yes honey, I'm leaving, I'm coming in half an hour. Well ... if there's no traffic!" Before hanging up, he sees the number displayed. Unknown. He stops.

"Hello?" he answers.

"Yes Alan, it's Tom. Are you still in the office?"

"I'm about to go home, I'm waiting for the elevator."

"OK, I'm on the 10th floor with Christophe. Do you still have a few minutes? He wants to talk to you urgently. It shouldn't last long."

"Yes of course! Where is his office on the 10th floor?"

"Take the elevator, press the button '10 SOUTH-EAST', it's unlocked, I'll come to get you."

"All right, see you in a bit."

Alan and Tom arrive in Christophe's office.

"Have a seat, make yourself at home, Alan," Christophe says.

"Good evening, Christophe."

"I know it's only been a few days that you're on this project. What is your action plan to right the ship?" Christophe asks calmly.

"Well, I've started with an assessment. I'm currently catching up with departments managers, subsidiaries managers, and the main people who intervened on the project. At this point, my goal is to identify concretely the reasons why the project is not moving forward. Then I will be able to act on those reasons."

"Fine! But, this is not the first time I've heard that. I made commitments to the Group's President. We should already have provided subsidiaries with the tools they need to work effectively. Now we must do it quickly. I want you to be fully imbued with the strong time constraint we have."

Christophe pauses, looks at Tom and stares right back at Alan before continuing.

"Send me your action plan very quickly; I want to know how you are going to proceed. If you face any obstacle, let me know directly. I won't keep you any longer. Have a nice evening."

"Thanks! Have a good evening too," Alan responds.

Tom and Alan leave the office and move towards the elevator.

"Of course," Tom says, "do not alert Christophe without talking to me first."

"Sure!"

They separate as they leave the elevator. Tom returns to his office, Alan heads towards the exit of the building.

The next day, Alan continues the interviews. He goes to the test team manager, Yu's office.

"My team is responsible for validating the products before they are delivered to the subsidiaries," Yu says proudly. "We prepare and write the test plans, run them and establish the acceptance sign-off. Finally, we are supposed to meet with the other teams to decide if the product is okay to be delivered or not. We also test deliveries that come from the maintenance team. My main problem is that delivery dates to my team are constantly moving; so, very difficult to plan works! Often, under pressure, we can't take the time to run the whole test plan until the end. Then, deliveries pass to the user acceptance tests team and are simply rejected."

"Do you plan those activities you mentioned for all projects?"

"Yes, of course!"

Yu looks exhausted. His dark-ringed eyes suggest that he has not slept for several nights. He carefully takes off his big round glasses, cleans them slowly taking his time and puts them back on. He stares into space for a short moment and continues, gazing at Alan.

"My teams write test plans based on the specifications. But as specs changes all the time, test plans and R & D deliveries also slip. Since we work on several projects, it's a real headache."

"I understand, Yu! It must be very painful to manage."

"And, I haven't mentioned yet the very poor quality of our friends' deliveries. Difficult to estimate the time necessary to test them: they're so full of defects. It's like they develop, don't do either unit tests, nor integration test, and just send the product for validation. I've never seen such a thing."

"So, what are your expectations for this project?"

"This project highlights our low level of maturity in large project management. My hope is that it would be our chance to improve all our processes and, in the end, people understand what process respect means in a large company like ours. I am ready to contribute with all my energy. With your arrival, I feel less alone in this challenge."

Alan continues the interviews with the managers of 'Maintenance & Support' and 'Operations & Production' departments. They complain that they haven't been sufficiently involved. Like their other colleagues, they want the project to be an opportunity to improve project management processes within AssurTGE.

After all the interviews, Alan writes a summary, sends it to the people he has questioned and asks them to check for any errors or misunderstandings in the transcript of what they told him.

Based on the new information collected from stakeholders, he updates the file "StakeholdersRegister.doc". He begins to synthesize in a table structured as below, how to manage each group of stakeholders according to their interests and the influence they may have on the project.

Stakeholder	Interest and Influence	Impact	Strategies
Business Managers A	High interest, High influence (identified many potential risks), project supporter	High	Involve this group in the periodic risk review

Table 1-2. Stakeholder Analysis Matrix: progressive elaboration

He names it "Stakeholder Analysis Matrix", updates it as his analysis evolves and obtains the synthesis presented in Appendix 3. His electronic organizer displays a pop-up message reminding him that the weekly project review with the team will start in twenty minutes. Immediately, what Tom said during their last discussion comes back to his mind: *"I heard this morning that we're very far from being able to meet this deadline. And this worries me a lot!"*. He pauses while still thinking. *"Well! I need to understand quickly what is going wrong and find the solution to move forward ... But how? Anyway, we'll see!"*

5

Before heading into the meeting room, Alan consults his mailbox.

> *Alan,*
> *As I told you earlier, not having started using this Centragiciel's module is causing a lot of trouble to our customers and consequently to our results and our reputation. I really hope that now we will finally have it on time as announced by Christophe. We really count on you!*
> *Regards,*
> *F. Dros*
> *Customer Relationship Manager, AssurTGE*

It's the weekly project review time. The seven group leaders, the test manager and the production manager are present.

"Hello everyone!" Alan begins. "You must have received the invitations for this one-hour weekly meeting I've scheduled until the end of the year. A business representative will attend as well."

"An hour every week?! What would we discuss so long at these meetings?" Esin asks.

"You'll see, we'll have plenty of things to talk about together. Time will run short, very short, and could even not be enough sometimes. For example:

- ✓ We'll maintain a list of problems you encounter and define together action plans to fix them.
- ✓ We'll review the project risks together. I will come back on this later. It may be necessary to dedicate time for it, depending on the number of risks we will have to deal with, we will adjust.
- ✓ Sometimes, when the steering committee meetings approach, we'll validate together the documents I'll have prepared."

"So, a lot of things!" Esin says.

"Yes, I have listed these points in the invitations. Of course, every week I will update the agenda. For this first session, let's get straight to the point. Tom told me that in a month, you are planning to deliver an intermediate version into production but things seem to be not going well. Can you tell me a little more?"

The validation manager begins:

"For my side, from the tests we have run so far, many defects are raised and we're only half of our test plan. I will publish the test report at the end of the day."

"Without going into details," Alfan says, "when I estimate the remaining works, I do not see how we can complete them in such a short time. And I don't consider the correction of the defects yet."

"Well," adds Betty, "the fact is, without the classes the group Alpha is developing, my team can't complete his implementation. We have moved on without, but we must do many reworks to integrate the group Alpha part. So…"

"We're fixing the last defects raised", Gama says. "Sure, So, I think it'll be okay for my part!"

"In my group," Delly says, "we have developed only a half of the requirements and there is still the most complex to work on. I'm sure we cannot finish in such a short time."

“Hold on!” Esin exclaims, “Let’s make it clear to Alan. We need to explain this to him. He has just joined the project and doesn't know anything about its past. I heard that the work is initially estimated at six months for the entire team. And after that, they kept giving a new deadline. But where do their dates come from? From a hat?”

Esin pauses for a few seconds, breathes, and continues.

“I don’t want to be the one who is always unwilling. I have a family to feed and mortgage loans to repay! But, I need to be frank and direct. These works were very badly estimated! Considering what remains, obviously, we cannot deliver anything in a month! So, please, let's not be a hypocrite and say it frankly!”

It's Zely’s turn, the leader of the group Zeta.

“It's the same for me!” Zely adds. “I’ve also asked myself that question. Well, I remember, it's been a year now, uh ... what was his name again? your predecessor came to me with a list of requirements and asked for a rough estimation to develop them. We looked at them together for a few minutes, and I told him that at first glance it might take about six months of work for the whole team. And, I also told him that I’d need a little more detail on the requirements and time to refine the estimate. Well, since then, no news. And those delivery date’s postponements began.”

They continue the discussion and reach the conclusion that it’s not realistic to think they can deliver within a month, as expected. To date, a delay of about two months is expected.

Leaving the meeting, Alan immediately alerts Tom and Christophe by email. Christophe responds: “No way to change the date again, it's your challenge and I know you’ll get it!”

Alan goes down to see the Alpha group. Developers focus on investigations of performance defect but can’t find the root cause. He approaches Jeff, a senior developer, sitting in front of his screen.

"I know why you've come to me," Jeff starts, looking desperate. "We've been on it for a while. We've done a lot of analysis together; I continue to investigate. Let me show you."

Jeff keeps his eyes fixed on the screen. Alan stands next to him and watches him, silent.

"It will be very hard to reproduce!" Jeff says. "The defect doesn't occur systematically, it looks like an exception is raised in a twisted use case."

He continues to scan the codes and comments aloud. Alan still does not say anything.

"Oh, dear ... the codes are meaningless. Many blocks 'If then ...' nested inside each other, all with loops everywhere!"

He remains calm for a moment as if he is concentrating, then resumes.

"I think many developers have gone through this method and everyone has patched it up. And they don't even bother to add comments on their codes, those guys!"

He turns to Alan and points to the screen while talking.

"Look at this! Is this a method? It does everything, thousands of lines!"

He focuses on the codes, eyes firmly fixed on the screen.

"Uh, I forgot that one! It's everywhere!" he adds incredulously. "They access systematically the database in the loops! Honestly, the way this is coded, I'm surprised the application has worked till now."

"OK, can you manage?" Alan interrupts. "I've heard that you are the last resort to sort all that out!"

"I tell you, it will take time to find out the root cause. We'll need mass, well, I mean a lot of data in the base to reproduce the problem. I have to build a dedicated database for that. And it will take time, but I have no choice."

Jeff stops a few seconds, thinks, and continues.

"Then, I'll have to add traces to strategic places in the codes, and analyze them. All this is time-consuming."

"OK, good luck! Keep me updated", Alan says and goes back to his office.

Alan turns on his computer and starts writing a document. The desk phone rings, it's the test manager.

"The situation is getting worse!"

"That's to say?"

"An issue is preventing my team from continuing to run a number of test cases. Say, the most important."

"So testers are stuck, is that what you mean?"

"Correct! We have just raised a defect. It's important that developers unblock us quickly, otherwise, the delivery to prod will be later."

"OK, warn Alfan, the group Alpha lead. I will speak to him before our defects review."

Alan closes the document he was writing and looks in his mailbox. Many messages are waiting for him. He goes quickly through them one after the other then stops on the following:

> *Alan,*
> *I'm sending you this article from a reporter close to the chairman of Globalinrance's board of directors. As you can read, the pressure to start using our tool is not only internal to AssurTGE. We really count on you to have it on time as announced by Christophe!*
> *Regards,*
> *D. Lègres, Marketing Manager AssurTGE*

He suddenly feels lost and powerless against all these problems that all occur at once. *How to right this ship? I can really see it flowing slowly. But, I know I can do it. I'm convinced. Hang on, Alan!*

Very quickly, he organizes a catch up with all the managers including the business representatives. Together, they go through the defects and prioritize them. The developers still have not found the root cause of the bug that was degrading performance. The validation manager insists on the urgency of unlocking testers. They decide not to start developing new features and put efforts on resolving priority defects. They end the meeting realizing that the delivery is even more compromised than they thought.

As usual, Alan and Tom meet in a comfortable resting place to catch up.

"We are Friday," Tom says, "the situation is worse than I thought. What do you suggest?"

"Take a step back and do not panic. Above all, do not transmit our stress to the teams! It can make things worse."

"Oh? Do you think I'm panicking or stressed? What's your plan?"

"We stabilize the app and then we'll see a little more clearly."

Alan's cell phone rings.

"Excuse me two seconds, it's Yu calling, there may be some good news."

He gets up and turns his back on Tom.

"The teams have just alerted me," Yu says. "There isn't enough disk space on the server, and memory either. We can't do any performance test anymore. Can you follow me?"

"Sure, I can. Some test cases were blocked because of a defect and now your team is completely stuck due to that disk and memory problem."

"Correct. The problem is that it takes a whole week to prepare the server. You know, it's the IT process."

"A week!?"

"I'll let you guess the impact on our delivery. I'll do what is necessary; we'll talk about it again on Monday."

"OK! You're a messenger of bad news," Alan adds smiling, "don't call me back by then."

Alan hangs up and turns to Tom.

"What's that issue with disk and memory? Couldn't it be anticipated?" Tom asks.

"Certainly," Alan responds, "But it's like most of the other problems you've encountered so far."

"Let's move on," Tom says, "I'll let you handle it. I read the summary of the interviews you sent and I already have some feedbacks. The teams appreciated being consulted as you did. I feel that your approach has boosted them. So, how do you analyze all that?"

"I clearly see that they all want to work following a plan, a guideline. The project started too quickly. There was no clear and shared project plan that served as a reference. So, everyone is lost after a while. Without a roadmap well known to all, it's normal that people don't move in the same direction!"

"That's right," Tom admits. "And it's also true that we underestimated this project from the beginning. There are many people on it, but the resources are not used effectively either. So, what do you plan to do?"

"We still have a few years ahead to spend on the project. It's essential to reschedule the remaining works according to best practices by following proven planning processes. And then, we'll have a project plan that will guide us in the future."

"So, what will we do with the deadlines we have already announced and that are ahead of us? It's true that these deadlines were guesstimates and finger-in-the-air exercise. But there's no choice, we have to meet them, you see!"

"They are project constraints. By rolling out the planning processes the way it should be, we'll know the magnitude of the work that lies ahead and then, look for solutions and means up to that. To fight the enemy, one must know his strengths and weaknesses! Then, develop a combat strategy up to his strength."

"Well, I see you're in good shape. What are your famous magic planning processes?"

Tom's cell phone rings. He looks at his watch; it was 8 pm. He says goodbye to Alan, takes his stuff and moves quickly to the elevators.

The next morning, Alan, in a meeting with his team, seeking solutions to the problems the team encounters.

"Let's go back to our discussion about the next delivery," Alan begins. "We are backed up against the wall! We explored all the options. There's one left: make a hole in the wall and then go through."

"What do you mean by that? The hole in the wall," Alfan replies.

"Have you ever experienced overtime here?" Alan asks. "It will be necessary to motivate teams to work harder: work late and work on weekends!"

"I don't think my teams will be against that, as long as we pay extra, of course!" Betty responds.

"I must talk to them," Gama says. "But I think we can have many candidates for."

At the end of the meeting, the group leaders explain the idea to their teams. Some developers and testers are happy to work on Saturdays to boost their payroll. Others who cannot on Saturdays, suggest working until late on some evenings, happy as well to be paid for overtime.

Alan calculates the costs of the measure and quickly meets Christophe and Tom. He introduces the idea to them. Christophe validates it and asks to apply it the same day. Tom asks to put in place very quickly a system of control to track the works the teams will do on the weekends.

The developers continue to investigate the defect that blocks testers until late at night. They still don't find any root cause.

6

A few days later, Hana, the developer who works on the defect, catches up with Alfan, her manager.

"We've made progress," she says, happy. "I've found where it stuck. For now, I have no solution for a definitive resolution. But I know that the fix may take days. And it will impact several parts of the codes."

"So, a high risk of regression! A large number of tests to plan, you mean?" Alfan asks.

"Exactly!"

"Umm… and it will push the delivery back to an indeterminate date!" Alfan says, worried.

"Yes, but there is a workaround. To unblock the validation more quickly, we can add two parameters in a configuration file. Then make some adaptations in the codes. Obviously, this is only a temporary solution and we will have to find a definitive solution after delivery."

"OK, I'll talk to Alan about it, but I think it's a good idea."

Immediately, the group leader suggests the idea to Alan and he validates it. The developer starts working right after on this solution to test it as soon as possible.

Alan heads to the test team manager's office. He meets the lead of the group Beta.

"Have you made any progress in solving the performance problem?" Alan asks.

"We're still investigating; we haven't found anything yet!"

"All right, keep me posted."

Alan continues on his way and arrives in the test manager's office.

"Have you found a solution to the environmental problem?" Alan asks.

"I raised a ticket in urgent mode and I hope the IT support will respond quickly."

"Perfect! You should have received an acknowledgment by email; forward it to me."

Alan finishes going around the teams and goes back to his office. He receives the acknowledgment from Yu, adds a message recalling the urgency of the request and sends it to the IT head, adding Tom in copy. He calls the IT head but gets his voice mail and leaves him a message: "*Hi, this is Alan, the new AlphaProject's project manager. I'd like to alert you that I've just sent you a very urgent email. You can call me back for more details in case my message is not clear.*" Just after hanging up, he notes that Tom has reiterates his email to the IT head with Christophe in copy, emphasizing: "*indeed, this ticket is very urgent!*". Then, Christophe does the same by adding: "Thanks for your quick action!"

It's the end of the week. At the end of the day, Jeff, the developer who investigated the performance's problem, exclaims, very happy: "I've found it! The cause of the slowdown ... I've found!". He gets up and continues:

"Yes, I fucking got it! it kept me awake for nights. But, in the end, who has the last word? It's me!"

Some of his colleagues approach him, surprised by his cry of joy. Others take this opportunity to have a break and go get some air.

"Do you know what?" he continues, "it's a condition that is not met and the system enters in an infinite loop that causes the decline in performance. It's true that it's twisted, very twisted, that condition! But, I know where to make the change."

He spends his Saturday fixing the defect. He runs many tests and notices that there's an improvement even though a slight degradation which he hopes will be acceptable, remains in a specific use case. Very late on Saturday, he sends an email to his manager and Alan to announce the good news.

On Monday, at the end of the day, the test manager informs that the test environment is reinstalled and the team can restart working. Alan sends an email to the IT manager to thank him for speeding up the ticket processing.

Tom joins Alan in his office. They go to the cafeteria to take a break and discuss the next course of actions.

"Okay, we're quite back on track now! aren't we?" Tom asks.

"It's simple, we had estimated two months of delay, and now it's one. So, given the remaining amount of work, if we continue at this pace, we'll be only a month behind schedule."

"Considering where we come from, I'd say we're not so bad. But, if the teams work a little harder, they'll be able to deliver on time! That's what I'd like!"

Tom's phone rings.

"Yes Christophe, I was going to call you, we've just estimated only a month delay."

"What! A month? With all the extra resources I've injected? I was expecting better, two weeks delay max! Manage to bring that product out on time, it's a commitment!"

Christophe hangs up. Tom explains Christophe's reaction to Alan. They both go back to their offices.

Alan presses a button on his desk phone to listen to messages. He recognizes Diane's voice: "Alan, please call me back." He calls her back immediately.

"I got your message," he begins.

"Yeah, thanks for calling me back. I've just talked to someone on the validation team. Two important features are missing from the menu on the left."

"Are they in the specs?"

"Of course, they are! Both described on page eighty. I've also discussed with the developers. Apparently, they have been forgotten."

"Give me a moment, I'll check with the teams and recontact you."

"Okay, make sure they will be delivered; we will not be able to use the software without them. Something else. Did the product security manager contact you?"

"No."

"He has just said clearly that we can't put into production this module without adding new layers of security. There's a great risk of being hacked, with significant financial consequences! Given the urgency, I told him to contact you directly to discuss this."

"OK, I'll call you back."

Alan goes around the teams. Several key developers are off sick. Three days of leave for some, a week for others. He approaches the validation team area. Two testers are on sick leave there as well. One for two days, three for the other. The group's leads inform Alan that the developers are tense. They don't have time to go to lunch anymore. Unlike their habits, some order a sandwich and eat it in front of their computer, others just eat fruits accompanied with a coffee. As a result, they make many mistakes. Many repeat the same task several times. Each of them tries to recover his time lost and is not available to help the other.

This is the beginning of the week when they are supposed to deliver the first module. The atmosphere doesn't change. The team is understaffed. The work completely slows down. No progress at all. It's obvious, they can't deliver anything this week, it's now a fact! Worse, they lose the delay they had caught up, it's back to two months again! Alan can only alert very quickly. He joins Tom in Christophe's office.

"Two months late!? That is not acceptable! I understand that there were many sick leaves. Do manage to deliver in the next three weeks!" Christophe exclaims.

"Alan, why two months late?" Tom asks. "Didn't you say a month late?"

"Yes," Alan answers, "that was it, a week ago, when everything was better and the entire team was present."

Christophe's phone rings. Before answering, he concludes:

"I have another meeting in a minute, you know what I'm expecting from you! Good luck!"

Alan and Tom return to their respective office. It's late, Alan goes home.

A week later, developers and testers who were on leave come back. The team is now complete. Alan gathers all the groups and the validation teams together for a quarter of an hour meeting.

"I'm not going to take much of your time," Alan begins. "We haven't been able to deliver on time. Starting today, we have two weeks left to catch up and limit the breakage. It's a real challenge. I know that each of you is doing his best to ensure the project's success. Well, do continue these efforts, and work as a team. What will count in the end is the performance of the team as a whole and not your individual performance. I rely on you to meet this challenge together so that the product goes live in two weeks."

He pauses and asks if there is any question. Nobody responds and he continues.

"So… from today, each morning, in each group, you will spend fifteen minutes together to start the day. Each of you will speak about the problems he encounters. This will help to search for solutions together with your group leader for the rest of the day. Together, you will be stronger! You will also share with your group the activities you worked on the day before and the ones you plan to work on during the day. Your group leaders will help you to take advantage of these daily quarters of an hour."

He asks again if there's any question. Silence. He concludes and says good day to the team.

Right after, he brings together the business representatives, the test manager, the production manager and the product security manager.

"You all know the situation more than me," he introduces. "We must deliver in two weeks the part of Centragiciel that is being developed."

A business representative interrupts him and adds, "I confirm, since you failed to do it last week!"

Alan opens a document, projects it on the screen and continues.

"Here is the list of all that remains to be done. If we must do all of them, it's clear that we'll work another two full months minimum. My goal is that, together, we identify and prioritize the absolutely necessary requirements that make it possible to start using the product in two weeks. I know this is a very difficult exercise because we'd like to have everything at once. But together, if we take a step back, we can do it."

"Particularly, since other deliveries will follow soon after," the validation manager adds.

Together, the team reviews each defect and selects the ones that make the product unusable. They confirm that it's essential to add a security layer because the risk of piracy is too high. The group leaders ensure that they will find a workaround achievable on time. They agree to postpone the development of one of the two missing features because implementing them is likely to introduce regressions. At the end of the session, Alan sends an email to the participants recalling the decisions made.

Every morning, Alan meets with the group leaders and the validation manager after they have met their respective groups. Each manager talks about his problems, what his team achieved the day before, and what his team should work on during the day. Together, they find solutions to move forward.

Day after day, the teams progressively regain their motivation. They are more relaxed and help each other. Developers and testers who have chosen to work until late evenings continue to do so. Those who worked on the weekends maintain their rhythm.

It's the delivery week, the production manager and his team work closely with the developers and the validation team to prepare and validate the production procedures. In the middle of the week, Alan prepares the list of remaining defects and organizes a meeting with all the teams to officially decide whether the software has the green light to go into production or not. All participants approve the go live.

This is the D-Day. The production manager and his team finish the installation and inform Alan, Tom and Christophe. Christophe sends an email to all the teams and thanks them. Tom and Alan do the same and meet in a resting area.

"Phew! Finally," Tom says all proud. "It's well delivered, but with two weeks late, however! And now…?"

"Now," Alan responds confidently, "we'll learn from all the mistakes and the problems we've faced and improve ourselves!"

In the late afternoon, Alan is chatting with a group leader in his office. His mobile phone rings. He immediately picks it up. It's Tom.

"Alan, what's going on? Germany and Italy subsidiaries directors have just called me. It seems that after half an hour of use, Centragiciel's screens freeze and users can't do anything. That new version has brought some regressions in the software! Didn't you have it tested before putting into production?"

"Of course, everything has been tested!" Alan answers. "Let me check with the teams and re-contact you!"

"OK, fix it right now! Otherwise, switch the production back to the previous version immediately. I have to go back to a meeting," Tom says.

Alan picks up his desk phone and calls the person in charge of the validation.

"Yes, Alan," Yu answers.

"Are you aware of what users are saying?"

"Yes, I've been online with some of them for long. During the tests, we didn't notice the behavior they're describing at all. The user acceptance team did not observe that either. And weird, we can't reproduce it in our environment! The developers must investigate. Something is wrong!"

"Yeah…"

The group leaders get together with the developer Hana. They don't find anything which explains the behavior users are describing. They continue the investigation for hours. Alan joins them.

"That's really curious," Alfan says. "It doesn't occur in the validation environment."

"Have you checked the version number?" Alan asks.

"No ... That would just come from there?" Hana says incredulously. "Let's check anyway!"

Alfan connects to the production, compares the version with the one in the validation environment and exclaims:

"Unbelievable! What happened? The versions are not the same! The one in prod is not the good one, it's a version before the final!"

Alan looks at him, surprised.

"So, this is not the last validated?" Alan asks.

"Well, no, this is not the last validated! I don't know what happened."

Very quickly, Alfan alerts the production manager. Together, they inform users and deploy the right version. And everything works well...

"There was a real mistake somewhere!" Alfan says.

"I can see that! Now, we have to find what caused this ... and learn from it!" Alan concludes.

Alan, on the way back to his office, meets Tom who was heading to a video conferencing room.

"I've seen the conditions under which the teams have worked, with the result we know!" Tom begins. "It's obvious that they can't keep this pace throughout the project. There's room for improvement!"

"Indeed," Alan replies, "we must discuss this tomorrow!"

7

Alan and Tom walk briskly along the bridge connecting the North-West building to the South-East building and discuss the project next steps. Alan has a firm gait and looks confident, as proud to have met the first challenge. His face exudes his determination not to quit and go all the way. Tom begins to be convinced of the idea of rescheduling the remaining works but still fears for ongoing commitments.

"I understand," Tom says, "we better get the project back on track now before it's too late. But how are you going to proceed? You still have not explained. What does this mean workload wise?"

"I have to work with the teams and document how to manage the project. This document will serve as a reference. So, it must be shared by all. I need to create it from the team's inputs. We aren't going to do it all in one go, but iteratively."

"Is that what you were calling 'Project Management Plan'? Isn't it just a new schedule then?"

"Exactly! The plan is more than just a schedule."

"Will you need to get the teams out of the activities they're currently working on? It would further delay the project. Why don't you create it yourself?"

"To make it realistic and make sure it's adhered to, I have to involve the teams in its elaboration. Otherwise, we will have beautiful processes well described but no one will follow."

"OK, something else. You know, we don't have visibility on the entire scope of the project," Tom recalls. "Many features still need to be elucidated."

"Well! I will plan workshops. One of them will focus on requirements elaboration. They will take place in small working groups."

"Hum," Tom says, worried. "Will you need developers in these working groups? I prefer to avoid that because they are currently working on tasks that will allow us to meet our commitments."

"No, not all! But some major developers will have to participate. Their participation will help develop a plan which is as realistic as possible."

"All this will consume a lot of resources and put us even further behind! My main concern is more about developers' time."

"You'll see, they won't all participate. In addition, not all activities require a workshop. As soon as I plan them, we'll have a clear view of the impacts on current developments."

"OK, I look forward to seeing that."

Alan goes to his office, turns on his computer, and starts working on the plan.

A developer joins him.

"Hello Alan, my group's leader is off today, may I disturb you a second?"

"Yes, of course, how can I help you?"

"I would just like to work without being interrupted every minute by network connection problems. We're already late. If in addition, our tools break down continually, it won't help."

"Be more specific, Joras! What's the problem?"

"Our servers started slowing down like I can't believe since this morning and we're disconnected almost every ten minutes. It's impossible to work in these conditions."

"Have you contacted the IT guys? Or open an incident?"

"Of course, but they don't know yet the origin of the problem, they're investigating."

"Give them some time for investigation, then. Try to do other tasks in the meantime."

Alan continues his planning activities until the end of the day.

The next day, he meets Tom again and shows him the workload the replanning will require.

"As you can see," begins Alan, "in addition to the group leaders, only four developers will participate in the workshops."

"I see."

"I've chosen the developers so that I can minimize the impact on the project by considering the criticality of the activities they're working on and by avoiding the most critical resources."

"What's the impact on the current schedule?"

"One-month delay."

"Only!?" Tom exclaims, surprised. "I was expecting more. Are you sure of your schedule?"

"Sure! This is because most of them work on parallel activities and especially not on activities that determine the end date of the project."

"Given how tough it was to deliver recently," Tom says relieved, "it's perfectly justified. So, start with the workshops that have the least impact on developers' time. For the rest, we'll have to convince Christophe."

"Yes. If we don't take any action to bring the project back on track soon, we already know that all our deliveries will be late, very late! In addition, the expected and required quality of deliverables won't necessarily be achieved. If we make this effort of reappraisal, we'll remove problems of misunderstanding of the needs and we'll deliver according to the new references time, quality, and cost. Personally, putting the project under control is essential, it's clear!"

"Perfect! At the end of your replanning phase, we'll know the truth about your famous new references then?"

"Exactly!" Alan answers, happy to have convinced Tom.

"So, prepare the plan and we'll present at the next steering committee meeting."

Alan's smartphone beeps. He gets a look at it, It's the SMS from the manager in charge of the functional domain "Management": "*Yum-yum, I'll pick you up in five minutes.*"

It's time for the requirements workshop. All business representatives are present in the meeting room. The test manager and group leaders are also invited.

"Alan, Laura is an expert user of our applications," a business manager says. "I've asked her to join us for this workshop. She will represent the users."

"Excellent idea!" Alan replies, then moves on.

"First of all," he says, "thanks for being on time for our first workshop. As you know, in each of the functional domain, some requirements still need to be defined, others to be clarified. During these sessions, we'll specify them. I'd like us to work in a group because some of the requirements can be overlapped and need to be discussed together. Afterwards, you'll organize parallel workshops for each business domain with your respective teams to deepen them. But first, a few reminders. We're going to start with the *functional requirements.*"

“That’s to say the functions expected of Centragiciel,” Flavienne, one of the business representatives, interrupts. “Is that right?”

“Exactly! Just think of the services you want Centragiciel to provide to the users by imagining that they are using it. A functional requirement is what Centragiciel has to DO.”

“For example, ‘create a client record’. Is that correct?” Flavienne asks.

“Correct!” Alan answers. “It's that simple! But we must also think about the services that Centragiciel has to provide without a user explicit request. For example, when a phone call arrives, it will automatically search for caller information and display it on the screen.”

“Indeed, that's an action from Centragiciel. It can react to events, it’s smart! Well, I didn’t think about these types of services. I focused on requests from users!”

“Something else,” Alan says. “Requests for services may also come from a ‘non-human actor’”.

“Non-human actor?” Flavienne asks.

“Yes,” Alan insists. “For example, a request that comes from our partners’ software or any other system.”

“Oh yes ... that's right!” Flavienne says. “This will be the case when every evening, our agencies systems will have to inject in Centragiciel the subscriptions of the day.”

“And maybe also Centragiciel needs to exchange information with suppliers, partners, etc. We must think of all this! Is that okay? Are you following?” Alan asks.

Participants respond, “perfectly!”

“Basically, a service that a human can ask Centragiciel, another system can also ask it,” Flavienne comments.

"Yes," Alan answers. "We could call 'Actor' a human user or a system that can interact with Centragiciel. This is often done by people who draw diagrams to represent use cases."

"OK, it's clear!" Flavienne says. "Do you know that Centragiciel has several modules? There's the module 'Management' to manage our partner's records, our customers, our suppliers, and our campaigns. The module 'Agencies management' is dedicated to the management of our agencies. 'Human Resource', often referred to as 'HR', helps to manage the records of all AssurTGE employees and its subsidiaries. 'Repository' is a huge knowledge base of our business that will be filled as users use the other modules. Finally, 'Support' is reserved for support activities for our agencies, our partners, our customers and our suppliers."

"Sure," Alan answers, "I read this in the document you sent me. And many needs are cross-functional and grouped in one module."

"Exactly! That's why it's a good idea to work together in this first workshop," Flavienne remarks.

"Ok, let's start with modules," says Alan.

Alan gets up and goes to the board. He draws six circles well-spaced from each other and writes in each of them the titles of the modules. He pursues.

"The aim of the game is to list around each module the actions that an Actor can request from Centragiciel or a service that Centragiciel can provide to an Actor. To be quick and not miss ideas, I suggest that you use at first, just infinitive verbs like 'Consult', 'Order', 'Pay' etc. to list these actions. Then, we'll go back over each of the actions to detail them if necessary. Understood?"

"Yes," Flavienne answers. "Well, that means we'll proceed iteratively!"

"Each participant will note the ideas of the module for which he is responsible."

“OK, we can start!” Alan says.

“For the module ‘Cross-functional’”, Flavienne begins, “I see: ‘Search’, ‘Access’, and ‘Customize’.”

Alan draws three lines starting from the circle ‘Cross-functional’ and writes on top of each of them the actions listed by Flavienne.

Laura, the user representative, suggests:

“For the module ‘Management’, I would simply say ‘Analyze’, ‘Create’, ‘Modify’, ‘Qualify’, ‘Validate’, ‘Order’ and ‘Pay’.”

Alan draws seven lines from the circle ‘Management’ and writes on each, the listed actions.

“For ‘Support’,” Diane intervenes, “you can simply note ‘Assist’.”

Alan draws from ‘Support’ a line on which he writes ‘Assist’.”

He pauses for a few seconds, observes the circles and lines he has just drawn and continues:

“Let's see what we get in the form of a table. A participant then displays the following table 1-3:

Module	Branches
Cross-functional	
	Access
	Customize
	Search
Management	
	Analyze
	Create
	Update
	Qualify
	Validate
	Cash
	Pay
Support	
	Assist

Table 1-3. Progressive elaboration of requirements: features list by modules

Thus, the participants list the first level of actions expected from Centragiciel.

"Have you noticed?" Alan continues, "I drew a line for each of the actions each time you list them. Consider each of them as the branch of a tree, the one that represents what is expected from

Centragiciel. Now we're going to detail each of them a little more by creating sub-branches."

"Oh yeah ... And the trunk of the tree would be the module!" Flavienne adds with a smile.

"That's it!"

Flavienne amuses herself by drawing on her notebook a tree whose trunk is the module 'Cross-functional', with three branches and sub-branches to materialize Alan's idea.

"OK, but what level of detail do you want?" Flavienne asks.

"As you can! It can be a simple verb like we did earlier or a sentence. We'll see later how to formulate our requirements. Just be brief! For now, just search for feature ideas! To make it easier, I suggest that we proceed module by module. Can we start with the module 'Support'? It has only one branch: the branch 'Assist'."

"Good idea!" Diane responds. "Well, for that branch, creates the sub-branches 'Save the incoming phone calls', 'Save emails', 'Save SMS messages'."

"OK," Alan says. "You mean information coming from all communication channels, I guess."

"That's correct!" confirms Diane.

Alan draws an oblique line from the line 'Assist' and writes above 'Save the information from communication channels'.

"Then add the sub-branches 'Create client file' and 'Route the caller'," suggests Flavienne.

"Uh ... And 'Show sender or caller record'," Laura adds.

Alan draws the sub-branches suggested.

"OK, can we move to the module 'Management'?" Alan asks.

Laura suggests the first ideas: "For 'Management', the branches 'Analyze', 'Create', 'Modify', 'Qualify', 'Validate', 'Order' and 'Pay' were listed. Under 'Analyze', I would put the sub-branches 'Save history of changes' and 'Track user activities'."

"I would add: 'Show predefined queries', 'Make custom queries' and 'Generate graphs'," Flavienne says.

Alan creates the sub-branches listed. Each module manager continues to update the structure in his table as the workshop progresses.

"In fact," Diane intervenes, "when I said 'Create' for the module 'Management', I was thinking of 'Create Prospect records', 'Create Purchase records', 'Create Customer records' and 'Create Supplier records'."

"OK, 'update' and 'delete' them too. No?" Alan asks.

"Yes, 'update' them, but not 'delete' them," Diane answers.

"Perfect!" Alan says.

Alan creates the sub-branches for creating and updating records.

"Oh ... I've forgotten!" Flavienne says suddenly. "There's also the management of documents such as purchase orders and quotes. We have to be able to 'Generate', 'Edit' and 'Upload' them."

Together, they complete the previous table and Alan displays it to all participants.

"So, with the sub-branches," Alan says, "it gives ..."

Modules	Branches	Sub-branches
Cross-module		
	Access	
		Authenticate
	Customize	
	Search	
Management		
	Analyze	
		Save change history
		Track user usage
		View predefined queries
		Make queries
	Create	
		Create Purchase records
		Create Prospect records
		Create Customer records
		Create Vendor records

Table 1-4. Progressive elaboration of requirements: features breakdown

(Part 1)

Modules	Branches	Sub-branches
	Update	
		Update Purchase records
		Update Prospect records
		Update Customer records
		Update Vendor records
	Qualify	
	Validate	
	Cash	
	Pay	
	Manage documents	
		Create
		Edit
		Upload
Support		
	Assist	
		Save channels information
		Create member records
		Forward caller
		View sender or caller records
Etc.		

Table 1-4. Progressive elaboration of requirements: features breakdown (Part 2)

Participants continue this way and break down all branches when necessary.

8

"Now," Alan begins, "we'll be able to formulate the requirements. Obviously, these are just the most detailed features, so those that appear at the last level of the table, in our case, sub-branches. First, let's agree on how to formulate them."

"OK! Is there a trick for that?" Flavienne asks.

"We'll just write them in a simple sentence following the template <subject> <verb> <complement>," Alan replies. "The complement says the 'What?' and the verb describes the expected action. Example: From our sub-branch 'Authenticate', we'll simply write a sentence like: 'The software must be able to authenticate a member using his membership card'. In this example, 'Software' is the subject, 'authenticate' the verb and 'a member...' the complement. You'll put 'must' when you already know that the requirement is mandatory, otherwise, simply put 'should' or 'could' if you want to recommend one possibility among others. Anyway, we will do a workshop dedicated to requirements prioritization. So, don't waste too much time on it now."

"Perfect! It seems clear to me!" Diane says.

"You can use the following wording as well," Alan adds.

He writes on the board while reading aloud:

"As <ROLE> I want <feature or action> for <REASON indicating profit for the software>".

He walks two steps towards the participants and continues the explanation.

"Can you notice that? We answer the questions 'Who?', 'What?', and 'why?'".

He pauses, thinks for a few seconds, looks for an example and continues:

"Still with the same example as before, you could write: 'As an agency operator, I want to authenticate to log in to Centragiciel'. To give you another example, let's take the sub-branch 'Create Purchase records'. It'd lead to, 'As an agency operator, I want to create the purchase records to submit a request to the purchasing manager.'"

"It's true that these formulations are simple and precise," Diane remarks.

"So, if my explanations are clear, I suggest that we formulate some of them together and then, each business domain manager specifies his requirements with his team after the workshop."

All participants accept the proposal. They define some requirements and get a list an extract of which is below:

- ✓ The software must be able to authenticate a member using his membership card.
- ✓ The software must record the history of the dates and authors of changes made on data.
- ✓ The software must have indicators that measure a member's use of his personal space: the number of connections in the year, date of last connection, list of modules consulted and their number of consultations.
- ✓ As an agency operator, I want to create the Purchase records to submit a request to the Purchasing Manager.
- ✓ As Purchasing Manager, I want to validate the Purchase records to authorize execution of payment.

- ✓ As an agency operator, I want to edit a Prospect records to update its information.
- ✓ As an agency manager, I want to qualify the Prospect records to change the status of the prospect.
- ✓ The software must be able to generate a PDF format on the screen.
- ✓ The software must allow users to edit a PDF document and modify it.
- ✓ The software must allow users to upload a PDF document to their documentary base.
- ✓ The system must automatically route the call to an experienced agent when the caller's case involves litigation or the person is identified as a VIP.
- ✓ The software must automatically display a form to create the caller's record when he is not identified in the database.
- ✓ The software must automatically record in its database, information from the various channels used by customers to contact agencies: email, internet, mobile internet, telephone, fax, SMS.
- ✓ The software must provide input help; for example, to propose the names of cities or towns that are attached to a postal code.
- ✓ The software must automatically pre-populate the caller's known data when it is identified.
- ✓ The software must automatically display a member's record when the caller is identified.

"OK," Alan says, "let's move on to another type of requirement: *non-functional requirements*. Do you remember? I said at the beginning of the workshop, speaking of a *functional requirement* that it describes what Centragiciel must DO. Well, the *non-functional requirement* specifies what it needs to BE!"

"Indeed," Flavienne adds, "this is where we will talk about its ergonomics, performance and ease of use, I think."

"Well spotted!" Alan confirms. "First, we will list the non-functional points to explore, then we will specify some requirements together and finally each business manager will continue the work after the workshop. Who starts? Flavienne has already mentioned a few."

"Well," Laura answers, "we can add to Flavienne's list: the user interface, the customization of languages and currencies, accessibility, execution speed, reliability, availability, robustness and scalability."

"And also," Yu adds, "the compatibility with versions of operating systems and database management systems, or more generally the technical environment where Centragiciel is going to be installed, as well as types and versions of browsers."

"There's also interoperability with other systems, constraints related to data migration and security," Flavienne adds. "In fact, we often encounter these types of requirements. So, we have already listed almost all in the existing docs."

"OK, for each of these points, let's specify the requirements now," Alan suggests. "An example for ergonomics?"

"Yes," Flavienne starts, "the user interface layout is important for us and followed closely by our Marketing Department. So, 'the interfaces must comply with each subsidiary's graphic charter'."

"And the novelty: quick access," Diane adds. "Centragiciel should provide a quick access from the home page to the four main features common to the subsidiaries."

"Can you find one about the ease of use and the accessibility?" Alan asks.

Diane looks at the other business representatives and answers:

"It has already been specified that 'Centragiciel should be easy to use for users who have completed four hours of training'."

"About availability, it's already specified that 'the software must be available between 6:00 am and 10:00 pm, local time of each country in which it's used,'" Laura says.

"It seems that I haven't seen anything about the speed," Alan says.

"Well, it's simple," Laura answers very quickly: 'It must have a response time of less than two seconds at startup and about millisecond during navigation'."

"For the scalability, I already mentioned that 'it must be able to serve simultaneously 150,000 users from 6:00 to 12:00, local time and 100,000 from 12:00 to 22:00,'" Flavienne adds. "And to give an idea of the total number of potential users, I also added that 'it must be able to manage 500,000 users during the first 6 months after the start of production, and 800,000 users later'."

"Perfect! Did you think about robustness?" Alan asks.

"Oh ... no! Well, it should continue to work properly in offline mode if the link with the central server is cut," Flavienne says.

Participants list the non-functional requirements as listed below:

- ✓ The software must have a response time of less than 2 seconds at startup and about millisecond during navigation.
- ✓ The software must be able to serve 150,000 users simultaneously from 6:00 am to 12:00 pm local time and 100,000 from 12:00 pm to 10:00 pm.
- ✓ The software must be available between 6:00 am and 10:00 pm local in each country in which it's used.
- ✓ The software must be able to manage 500,000 users during the first 6 months after the start of production, and 800,000 users later.
- ✓ The software should continue to work properly in offline mode if the connection to the central server is down.

- ✓ The interfaces must comply with each subsidiary's graphic charter.
- ✓ Centragiciel must provide fast access from the home page to the 4 main features common to the subsidiaries.
- ✓ The software package should be easy to use for users who have completed 4 hours of training.

Alan merges each business manager functional requirements tables, completes the list obtained with the non-functional requirements and together they browse it. He reminds them that business managers will have to add to this, the list they will elaborate with their respective teams.

"Perfect!" Alan exclaims. "We have now come to the end of the first part of the workshop. But, just for information, the work on the requirements is not really finished. System requirements still need to be specified. They are rather technical and elaborated during the system technical design based on the business requirements. So, the technical teams will take care of them at the appropriate time. This is not the purpose of our workshop."

"Great, I think we've done a good teamwork!" the test manager says.

"I confirm!" Alan adds. "Now, we have to define the acceptance criteria for each requirement."

"Yes, that's it!" Diane says. "Yu, our 'Quality' guy will be of great help on this point."

"It's late now and I think we'll be fresh and efficient by getting on it tomorrow morning. What do you think?" Alan asks.

All participants answer 'yes, absolutely!' One of them adds: "Let's continue tomorrow morning while the requirements are still fresh in our heads. Alan, you did well to book two days."

"Thanks all and see you tomorrow nine am," Alan concludes.

It's 6 pm. All participants rush back to their office to check their emails and go home. Alan approaches the boards, photographs them with his smartphone and puts away his phone. He returns to his place, puts his fingers on his computer keyboard and quickly types a series of keys to lock it. He stares into space for a few moments as if thinking of something: *At this late hour, who will come to start a meeting? After all, I can stay here without disturbing anyone. It makes me a huge boss office all to me, I love it!*

He leaves the computer in the empty room, goes to his office, and consults his desk phone. It is flashing to announce missed calls. The screen displays twenty-six calls. *I did well to put my cell phone in silence! Otherwise, I would have been disturbed throughout my workshop.* He presses a key to see the first call. It was a manager who was trying to reach him, but didn't leave a message. He goes on to the next call, it came from Tom. Then, he begins to ask himself questions: *Strange, why is he trying to reach me? I warned him that during the workshops, I wouldn't be reachable. Is there something urgent?*

A few seconds later: *Ah ... he left a message*: "Alan, you should have received my email and the messages I left on your mobile phone. I had a big talk with Christophe this morning. Someone probably told him about the re-planning plan you are preparing. Even before we present him the details, he is already totally against that! For him, there is no question of rescheduling. He wants both of us to meet him, tomorrow at 8 o'clock in his office." He stops on this message, turns his head away from the station, turns around his desk and sinks into his seat. Moments later, he listens to the message again carefully.

He picks up the handset and calls Tom back to the office. No answer. He calls him on his cellphone. After the third ring, he gets the answering machine. Not knowing what to say, he hangs up without leaving a message.

He then heads back to the meeting room. Night is falling, the building has gradually emptied of its employees. A few small groups of two or three people are still chatting here and there in the office aisles. Arrived in the meeting room, he picks his laptop and returns to his office. On the way, he remembers Tom's message. The part "he is already totally against" is looping in his head like the refrain of a good song listened early in the morning. Except, in the current case, that is not about a song!

He goes into his office, pulls a seat, places it in front of his whiteboard and sits down. A few seconds later, he tilts the back of the seat slightly backward, crosses his arms to feel comfortable and begins to think while staring at the board. After a few minutes, he suddenly gets up, picks up a rag and automatically wipes the board for a long time until it shines. Then he returns to sit exactly in the same position he was before getting up.

Many questions cross his mind: what to do now? How can I prepare for tomorrow's meeting? How can I convince him? Progressively, a few snippets of answers come to his mind: I was already preparing the plan for the next steering committee scheduled in a month. I will put on the table the impacts of the new planning on current milestones, measure the risks we take if we don't reschedule, what we earn by doing it, and propose options. Without measuring, we will continue in the blur, and it will be difficult to make correct decisions! The planning process is still ongoing and I won't know the truth until it's completed.

Suddenly, he gets up, approaches the telephone, and begins to scroll through the rest of the missed calls: there were several calls from Tom and Chris, the R & D manager. Standing, looking out through the window, he whispers: "I'll sleep on it!"

The next day, it's 7 o 'clock am. He arrives at the parking lot and sees Tom's car. He takes the elevator and joins him in his office.

"Hey, Alan!" Tom exclaims as he sees him coming.

"Hi Tom, how are you since yesterday?"

“Not bad! Make yourself a coffee, you’ll need it. Christophe is not convinced of the need for your ‘rescheduling’. I think he imagines that you will end up announcing that it will be necessary to postpone the deliveries. And especially that, he’ll have to extend the budget. That's what I felt while talking with him yesterday. So, you have to convince him!”

Alan makes himself a coffee and sits comfortably.

“It's simple,” he says, “I'll see clearer when we have finished establishing the picture of the remaining works and their estimate. Without that, we don’t have real data and we can’t know if there will be a delay or not, an impact on the budget or not. All that must be assessed to have a clear view. Any long discussion without this step would be a waste of time.”

“Sure, I understand, but you have to sell your plan to Christophe.”

Tom's phone beeps. He looks at the screen: “Tom, I have to postpone our meeting, I'm summoned urgently by the Globalinrance vice president this morning. There’re rumors in the press that the delay of AlphaProject may affect the financial performance of the group and shareholders are worried. I'll call you back”. The message is signed Christophe. He turns to Alan, looking relieved.

“OK, both good and bad news! I let you read,” he said, handing to Alan his phone screen.

Alan approaches and reads the message.

“Hum ...” Alan says. “There’re leaks and rumors are already spreading in the press about a possible delay. Unofficial information is circulating in the media. There is room for improvement in our communication plan.”

“I'm afraid these rumors are premonitory,” Tom says.

“I need to speed up the planning activities. I need to go,” Alan answers. “The next workshop will start soon. We will prioritize the requirements and define the acceptance criteria. Keep me informed as soon as Christophe recontacts you."

"Oh? Prioritize requirements!?" Tom exclaims. "I know the teams well, everything is a priority for them, you'll see! Do you have effective techniques to do it?"

"Ah ... that! If you want to discover them, join us!" Alan answers, laughing, before rushing to his office.

9

Alan arrives in his office. As soon as he sits, he uploads to his computer all the pictures (the branches and sub-branches) he took during the workshop, selects some of them and integrates them into the requirements document he started. He goes through it, refines the layout and exclaims: “Great! Good doc! It contains all the requirements that can be defined according to the current state of knowledge of business needs. Now, all we need to do is to ask the business representatives to prioritize them.”

He gets up, stretches, and looks through his office window. He takes advantage of this pause to gaze for a long time at the beauty of the rays of sunshine that illuminate the gardens and fountains in the large AssurTGE courtyard. The show makes him revisit and re-experience his last vacation at the beach, on the shores of the Mediterranean with his wife and twelve-year-old daughter. The gentle wind, the smell and the calmness of the sea were relaxing him when suddenly he notices a presence behind and turns around. Flavienne.

“Hi, Alan!”

“How are you, Flavienne?”

“Good! I wanted to tell you yesterday. I find this workshop interesting; working as a team is rewarding. Thank you for the idea!”

"Indeed! This helps to be effective; in addition, it's friendly. We'll continue later."

"Yeah, it's almost time. I'm going to the meeting room."

"Wait, let's go together," Alan says, all satisfied.

It's 9 o'clock, all the participants settle in the room. Alan projects the document he has just formatted.

"Well, before starting to work on the acceptance criteria of the requirements, I propose to prioritize them first," he introduces.

"Prioritize them? Anyway, we need all of them. What's the point of wasting time prioritizing?"

"Good question, Diane! We will prioritize them based on the benefit they will bring to Centragiciel as a whole! This will help us in the future to know the requirements to be delivered at the earliest to meet users' needs in time!"

"Ah, perfect! Deliver as we go along according to the business priorities. It's a good idea!" Diane recognizes.

"And it's mainly you, business representatives, who will define the priorities. I suggest the following technique called 'MoSCoW'."

"But, what does Moscow have to do with prioritization?" Flavienne says, laughing.

Participants burst out laughing. Alan smiles and continues.

"Sorry, it's an acronym for English terms! You will quickly understand when I describe it."

Alan goes to the board and writes while reading:

- ✓'**M**ust have': Must be delivered
- ✓'**S**hould have': Should be delivered
- ✓'**C**ould have': Could be delivered
- ✓'**W**ould like to have': Would like it to be delivered

"It's clever, I get it!" Flavienne says. "It's simple, so we'll rank the requirements in each of these four categories."

"It seems I understand too," Diane says. "But it would be good if you explain clearly what each category means to avoid any misunderstanding."

"Sure, I will!" Alan replies before continuing.

"'Must have' requirements are those that are fundamental for Centragiciel to work. In other words, without them, no Centragiciel or it will bring no value to the users!"

He pauses for a few seconds to give the participants time to assimilate what he has just said. Silence.

"OK!" Diane says, to break the silence.

Alan continues his explanation.

"'Should have' are the ones Centragiciel needs to work properly. They are essential. Their absence will require heavier or more costly ways to meet user's needs."

"Ah, I already see a lot in this case!" Flavienne exclaims.

"The 'Could have' ones bring a real value to Centragiciel. But they can only be implemented if doing this doesn't impact others. Finally, the 'would like to have' are requirements that would be nice to integrate if we could. They can be developed immediately or later."

"Are you still following me? As Flavienne said, you'll need to match each requirement with the category that corresponds to it."

"Yes, everything seems clear to me," Flavienne answers and turns to the other participants.

"What about you?" She asks.

Each of the other participants responds one after the other: 'OK for me!'. Very quickly, each one ranks his exigence with the category he considers matching.

"Just for information," Alan warns, "until the end of the project, I'll remind you to keep this prioritized list up-to-date. I will help you do this! It'll be our common database of what needs to be developed."

He puts his hands into the pockets, takes a few steps scanning the audience then continues.

"Now, back to the way to formulate what I call 'requirements acceptance criteria'. It's very simple. We'll describe in front of each requirement, the criteria which will let us know if the delivery meets our request. Yu, as 'Quality' guy, we're right there in your domain, can you explain what it consists of?"

"Of course!" Yu answers. "The wording is very simple, it's based on the requirement's ones. Take for example 'The software must be able to authenticate a member using his membership card'. We can list the criteria below:"

- ✓ Test authentication with a valid membership card: the member must access Centragiciel homepage.
- ✓ Test authentication with a card that expires on the test date: Centragiciel must reject the access request and show the user the reason for the rejection.

"Of course, dear business experts, it's you who know the criteria than anyone, so do not hesitate!" Alan adds.

"In my side, my requirements acceptance criteria are clear in my mind, so it will be quick," one of the business representatives notices.

Some other business representatives add all together: "the same".

"Great!" Yu laughs. "We'll finish this workshop at the speed of light then."

"OK," Alan says. "Let's begin with good habits at the earliest. So, I suggest we continue by following the order of priorities. We'll start with the 'Must' requirements, then we'll do the 'Should', then the 'Could', and we'll end with the 'Would'. We'll follow this order throughout the project, for all our activities and the successive deliveries!"

The team defines the acceptance criteria requirement by requirement until the end of the workshop.

"OK cool," Alan concludes, "the requirements are now clear, prioritized, and their acceptance criteria are well known. Thanks all for that great teamwork!"

They all get up, stand around the coffee machine in the meeting room. They comment for some time on the two days of workshops they spent together. They are proud of the work they have accomplished as a team and the result. Slowly, their chatting moves on a rugby match played last weekend and the poor performance of the national team, comparing their project team to a rugby team. They continue the discussion for a while, then gradually disperse.

Flavienne approaches Alan.

"In general, these kinds of techniques have a name. What is the name of the one we used yesterday to define the requirements?" She asks. I'd like to do some research on this to learn more.

"Good idea! Search then 'Mind-Mapping' on the Internet."

"Thank you very much for allowing this teamwork. Not easy to work together in this company. Everyone always wants to work in his corner."

"Yeah, I see. I often notice this in the companies I work with."

Alan returns to his office, browses through the document that contains all the two days' work, does some adjustments, and puts it in a folder on a server accessible to all teams. He then writes an e-mail that he sends to all participants asking them to review the document and send him their comments within 48 hours.

A few hours later, he receives feedbacks. Some ask to complete some requirements, others suggest new acceptance criteria and others ask to change a categorization (a requirement that was in the category 'Should' to put in the category 'Must'). He makes all the adjustments requested and finalizes the document: it's ready to be validated. He then writes the email below:

> *Hi all,*
> *The requirements document is ready for validation. Please, send me your validation confirmation Wednesday 12, end of the day at the latest. As a reminder, after that date, it will be considered validated. If you have any comment, please complete the attached sheet and send it to me.*
> *Regards,*
> *Alan*

He re-reads it, inserts all those who attended the workshops as a recipient with their line managers in copy and sends it. It's the end of the day, he goes home, looking tired.

The next day, he writes another specific document 'Project scope' to define the project's boundaries. He mentions the scope (beyond the business requirements of Centragiciel), the list of expected deliverables, the acceptance criteria of Centragiciel as a whole, what is not part of the project, the constraints and assumptions of the project. He sends it to the same persons and asks them to validate it as well.

A few minutes later, Tom comes to see him in his office.

"Alan, you wanted to see Christophe. We can do it right away if you have a quarter of an hour."

"Yes, let's go! He must clearly give the green light before I continue the workshops. Will he support my approach to reorganizing the project? He didn't call you since your last discussion on this topic. I want to know for certain!"

They both go to Christophe's office.

"Alan," Christophe begins, "I've been informed that you're preparing to reschedule the project. That's right?"

"Well, my idea is to work with the teams on what remains to be done, then define the scope really expected by users, its related costs and realistic delivery deadlines."

"What? The current commitments are not realistic?" Christophe asks, looking astonished.

"Referring to what we've just experienced for the last delivery," Alan responds, "the observation is clear. It took more than a year to complete a part that is supposed to take six months and is considered the least complex. My investigations showed that the project is underestimated. More seriously, some features are still missing. There's a real risk of user rejection."

"Yes," Tom adds. "Moreover, what is delivered is only partial. We had to accept a lot of temporary workarounds. The teams still have to find definitive solutions."

"Basically," Alan argues, "if we continue at this rate, knowing that it's a tiny part of the entire software that was delivered, we'll have to multiply by ten the duration and costs to fully complete AlphaProject. And, I'm not talking about the damage this will cause to the morale of the teams for future projects, given the conditions in which they ended up delivering!"

Christophe is silent and listens to Alan and Tom.

"What I really like in this process," Tom continues, "is that we'll finally know the real magnitude of the work that awaits us."

Alan and Tom are out of arguments. They look Christophe straight in the eyes and wait for his decision.

Silence.

Christophe thinks for a full minute which seems like an eternity and breaks the silence.

"When is the plan for?" he asks.

"Next steering committee, in a month," Alan answers.

"OK, keep me updated before!"

Tom and Christophe continue to discuss but on other subjects. Alan returns to his office, motivated more than ever to speed up the workshops.

He schedules two workshops in the shared calendar: one will be devoted to the definition of project activities and the other to the estimation of their costs. He adds the message below, puts some developers and business representatives in the mail, and sends the invitations:

Dear All,
As you might remember, we had jointly established a WBS (Work Breakdown Structure, see Appendix 4, figure 2.1) that structures AlphaProject scope of work.
I suggest now that we go further by defining the activities that derive from it and estimate their costs.
To be effective, please review the WBS and each of the requirements listed in the requirements document.
To prepare the workshop, I have created a Question and Answer document. In front of each requirement, mention your questions. The business representatives will respond.
We have 48 hours to complete that 'Q & A' step before the workshop.
***PS:** All documents are up to date in the project folder.*
Regards,
Alan

10

It's 2 pm. All the guests are sitting in front of their laptops around a table so they can see the pictures on the board. Alan stands up in front of the group. The workshop begins.

"We'll define the project activities," introduced Alan. "For this, we'll start from each component of the WBS."

He displays the WBS on the screen and quickly comments on the components of the first three levels.

"Let's take the components in the order, from left to right starting with 'Project Management'," Alan suggests.

"I think you're better than us in 'Project Management' to quickly list the activities related to it," a participant says, with a smile. "What if you complete them alone after the session? Especially, since there's not much to do in terms of project management. It's us, the developers, who do the job anyway."

"This is a pertinent remark Alfan. Well ... the first part of the remark. So, let's go to the component 'Specifications'. I will take care of 'Project Management'!" Alan concedes.

"Cool," Diane interrupts. "For the module 'Management', I am already detailing the requirements so that developers can understand my expectations better. And I think my colleagues are doing the same for the other modules. The activity for this component is simply: 'Detail the requirements of the module 'Management'."

"Perfect! I'd add the activity 'review and validate the module *Management* specs'," Alan says.

"Indeed, when I finish, the teams will comment and validate them," Diane confirms.

"You've got it, Diane. It'll be the same types of activities for the other modules," Alan concludes.

Representatives of other modules respond, "That's right!"

"Now, let's move on to the next one."

By doing this, from WBS component to WBS component, the team defines the activities as listed below:

- ✓ Detail the requirements of the module 'Management'
- ✓ Detail the business rules of the module 'Management'
- ✓ Review and validate the specs of the module 'Management'
- ✓ Detail the business rules of the calculation engine of the module 'Invoicing'
- ✓ Optimize and evolve the model of Centragiciel's classes
- ✓ Design and update Centragiciel's database
- ✓ Develop the engine of the module 'Purchase'
- ✓ Develop the requirements of the module 'HR'
- ✓ Adapt the deployment procedure
- ✓ Prepare the packaging
- ✓ Etc.

All the team helped to remember the activities necessary for the good execution of the project.

It's the end of the session, all the participants return to their office. Alan stays a few moments and adds project management activities to the list, shuts down his laptop and goes to his office.

He sits, opens the activities document, and starts scheduling them in the order in which they will be executed. He notices that some activities can't start before others and others can be done in parallel. Then, he identifies all those dependencies. Very quickly, he integrates the activities into his planning tool 'PPlan', and begins to link them according to their dependence. He is stuck on some dependencies related to the technology and asks a developer to join him. Together, they define the remaining technical dependencies.

He wonders what other resources he needs to complete the project, in addition to the collaborators who will work on the project. He quickly drafts the email below and sends it to the development team leads.

> *Dear All,*
> *For the rest of AlphaProject, please, send me the list of your hardware or software needs related to your respective development environments. This includes virtual or physical machine needs, or disk space on existing machines, need for new software tools, or license renewal. Thanks to reply by the latest, tomorrow afternoon. Do not hesitate to come to my office or contact me for more details.*
> *Regards,*
> *Alan*

He then writes an equivalent email to learn about the resource needs in the test and validation environments. He sends the email to the relevant managers.

He reviews the list of activities and asks himself the same question about the need for external suppliers or providers. He realizes that there is actually no in-house expertise to work on the developments and the configuration of the module "Invoicing". Only some specialized integrators approved by the software publisher hold these skills.

In the days that follow, the business representatives write the specifications for their respective domains and publish them. He organizes the review sessions with the group leaders and the test manager. Together, they make corrections to the specifications and validate them all.

The following week, the workshop on workload estimates begins. Long before the meeting, Alan had asked developers to re-read the requirements as well as the answers to their questions.

Participants sit around a round table; Alan too. Everyone made a coffee with the machines that are at each corner of the room. Alan starts the overhead projector, projects the list of project activities on a screen and introduces the session:

"We'll focus on estimates of the activities of the components 'Detailed Design' and 'Development'."

He opens the specification documents and throws a pack of cards on the table.

"OK, we're going to play cards all day long!" Alan jokes like to relax the participants.

"They are numbered oddly, your cards, we can't play belote with that!" Alfan remarks.

"Exactly! They are specific to our poker game," Alan explains.

"Poker?! Be careful," Ethan warns smiling, "I'm good at this game; you'll all end up poor when you leave here."

"For the record, do you remember the Fibonacci sequence?" Alan asks.

"Oh ... that's too old, to remember," Betty replies. "It dates right back to when I was in college or high school, I'll ask my kids."

"Well, let me remind you, then," says Alan. "To create it, you start from the list 0, 1. You obtain the following number by adding the last two numbers of the list between them. Got it?"

"Ah ... Yes ... I remember now," Betty says.

Alan writes on the board while reading.

"It gives 0, 1, **1 (= 0 + 1)** then 0, 1, 1, **2 (= 1 + 1)**, and 0, 1, 1, 2, **3 (= 1 + 2)**, then 0, 1, 2, 3, **5 (= 2 + 3)**, etc. The next number is always the sum of the last two of the list."

"By doing this, step by step," he continues, "you'll get the sequence of numbers 1, 2, 3, 5, 8, 13, 21, etc."

"Okay, why are you telling us that? What's your point?" Alfan asks. "I could invent you a series of numbers too!"

Alan arranges the cards so as to show the order of the numbers inscribed on each of them.

"You see? The numbers of the cards are the famous numbers of the Fibonacci series."

"Oh yes, that's true!" Ethan exclaims.

"Did you know?" Alan continues, "Scientists showed that this progress describes how some things of nature grow. For example, the growth of tree branches, seashells, rabbit populations would follow this progression. Even the size of the problems we face every day and the effort required to solve them would follow this same progression. Isn't that amazing?"

"Impressive!" Ethan replies.

"We'll use those cards to estimate our requirements. The workload (in a day for one person) of a requirement will, therefore, be one of the Fibonacci numbers," Alan explains.

Alan gets up, goes around the table, distributes a set of six cards whose values range from 1 to 13 to each developer, returns to his place and sits, then continue his explanation.

"For each module, we will proceed requirement by requirement. I will start by reading the requirement and give you some details when necessary. To be sure that we have the same understanding, you will ask me your questions if you have any. Do you understand now the importance of our Q & A sessions for the preparation of the workshop?"

"Sure! It's clear that, if it was only now that we had to start working on the requirements understanding, we would spend weeks or months to estimate them," Ethan adds.

"As soon as I say 'go'," Alan continues, "you'll raise the card which has the number corresponding to the estimate (in a number of days per person) to develop and test the requirement. It's important that you raise your cards simultaneously to avoid influencing each other. Are the rules clear?"

All developers nod.

"So, let's begin!"

Gama interrupts him.

"Excuse me, Alan. If I follow you well, in the end, we won't be able to give workloads like 4 man-days or 6 man-days since these numbers are not in the Fibonacci series. It's disturbing. Can you please explain what the purpose of that restriction is?"

"It wouldn't be just because the size of the problems and the effort to solve them would follow that Fibonacci progression?" Alfan asks.

"Not really," Alan responds. "The main reason is that it allows you to focus on the significant differences between the estimates and avoids being distracted by details that aren't useful and that may waste time. In fact, each turn, we will retain the value to which you'll all converge. If there's a wide divergence between your choices, we'll try to understand why and will re-examine the requirement then redo the estimate."

"Ah ..." Gama says. "It's necessary that our choices converge at the best otherwise we'll repeat the estimation until convergence. I now understand the importance of focusing only on significant differences between estimates. This series of numbers helps us to achieve that."

"Exactly!" Alan confirms. "To facilitate this, we'll estimate a simpler requirement first. It'll serve us as a reference to estimate the most complex. It'll be a bit like our unit of measure. For example, we'll say, 'the requirement Y is twice as complex as our reference requirement and therefore will take twice as long to complete'. We'll start with the one I consider to be the simplest. So, let's go now!"

Alan reads aloud: 'The software must be able to authenticate a member using his membership card.'

"That's true, this one seems easy to develop," says Alfan.

Short silence.

"No question?" Alan asks. "So, 'Go!'".

The developers raise their card simultaneously. They all choose a 2-value card.

"Great! Perfect consensus," Alan remarks. "As I said, for the rest of the session, you can refer to it to estimate the more complex requirements. This will help to go faster."

He writes this value in his document.

"Then, let's move on to the next," he suggests.

He reads aloud: 'The system must automatically route the call to an experienced agent when the caller's case involves litigation or the person is identified as a VIP'.

"Hum," Alfan whispers, "this one can be a little more complicated to develop. There will be a lot more work."

"No question?" Alan asks again.

He looks at each participant and says "Go". All the developers raise their cards. Alfan assigns the value 13, a developer assigns the value 3 and the others the value 2.

"That's interesting!" Alan says. "Alfan, could you explain why '13'?"

"The part 'when the caller's case involves litigation or the person is identified as a VIP' will require a lot of work. In fact, the technical layers that manage 'VIP' and litigation records are different at present. Unfortunately, they were not well designed to communicate with other modules. They will have to be adapted to meet this requirement. In the end, to develop it, we'll have to modify not only one brick but three and make them communicate."

"Oh yes," Betty admits, "this might not be so simple! That said, the redesign of the two layers, 'litigation' and 'VIP', is already ongoing and will be completed before we begin the requirement's implementation. You're right; they still need to be adapted".

"Therefore, there're only two layers to communicate; This changes the situation!" Alfan says.

"OK, let's repeat the estimation by the same process. Do you have any other question or comments on this?" Alan asks.

He pauses a few seconds and says again "Go". The cards are raised simultaneously. Most show a 5-value card, some a 3-value card. Alan records the number 5 in his document and announces the following requirement.

They do so for all the requirements. When they meet a requirement that requires a long discussion, they put it aside in a separate list to rework in another session. Thus, they make progress well and estimate 90 % of the requirements. They immediately plan another session to work on the remaining 10 %.

"OK, ladies and gentlemen, we're done for today. Did you like the session?" Alan asks. The developers nod.

"In fact," Ethan says jokingly, "I wouldn't say I made money on this poker game. I'll have to catch up this weekend by going to play the real 'poker', now that you've made my mouth water. If I lose, I'll send you the bill, Alan."

"No problem, I'll forward it to AssurTGE!" Alan says, smiling too.

While some throw themselves on the delicious treats next to the coffee machines, two others follow Alan who was heading to his office. One of them explains that he found this estimation method very collaborative and that the estimates should be made in this way for all projects. Moreover, beyond the estimate, it encourages teamwork and knowledge sharing among developers. The other adds that he prefers this to the so-called "top-down" method where the project manager gives, in his corner, "wrong" estimates that anyway can't be met since they are often far from the reality of the work to do. Alan explains to them that they could search for "planning poker" to learn more about that technique if they wanted.

Whereas all the group has returned to their office, Betty continues to talk to Alan.

"Planning poker!? So, this is really the name of this method?" she asks again.

"Sure!"

"People who name the techniques take risks sometimes without realizing it," Betty says, surprised.

"Why?"

"'Poker' is a money game and as in any money game, you can quickly become addicted and ruin your life. I mean lose your car, your house, all your belongings."

"What has this got to do with naming a technique 'poker'?"

"Well, you've just experienced it without realizing. What Ethan told you about 'poker' was not a joke at all. You've just awakened in him the old demon that's the real poker game he's been fighting against for years. He even followed detoxification treatment in a specialized association. Remind him of this by making him play a fake poker game, can only make him want it again: the recurrence is sure! You know, it's like a drug, he'll have fun this weekend!"

"Really?"

Alan stops a few seconds, thinks, turns to Betty, and adds:

"All our experiences of everyday life, including experiences in our professional life, can arouse or awaken in us any type of emotions and feelings (demonic or angelic). It's up to us to be in control of ourselves. Am I wrong?"

"You're probably right, but in the meantime, I think that poor Ethan will relapse tonight!" Betty insists.

The next day, Alan proceeds in the same way as with the developers to estimate the activities related to the tests, but this time with the testers and the validation manager. He consults the historical records from previous projects to complete the estimates of activities related to the other WBS components. Based on his own experiences, he estimates the workload of activities related to "Project Management".

He opens the document he started with his planning tool, adds to each activity the estimated workloads, allocates resources to each activity according to available capacities and integrates into the tool the public holidays and the planned holidays of each of the collaborators. The tool displays the project end date. "*My God! I can't announce this end date?*" he murmurs.

His phone rings, he answers. Tom.

"Alan, are we having lunch together?"

"OK, I'll pick you up at 12:30. Is that okay?"

"Perfect!"

Alan goes back to what he was doing. He looks for options to optimize the schedule and does many end-of-project date simulations.

Now, let's see how much all this will cost to us. He adds in its planning all the software and hardware resources, the suppliers, as well as their respective costs, then displays the total cost.

It's lunchtime, he joins Tom.

"I have received a very good feedback on the workshops, the teams appreciate. What's the next?" Tom asks.

"The risks!"

"Oh, yes! I've often heard that they must be identified, analyzed and so on. But, we'd still have to be able to recognize the real risks."

"Well, if we are not very inspired, we'll practice a technique to get the machine started. In addition, I will explain to the team how to formulate them and how to analyze them."

"Great, interesting!" Tom says, obviously seduced by his interlocutor's confidence. "I understand now why the teams like workshops, they learn a lot, I see."

11

To prepare the workshop on the risks, Alan connects to the shared server where information and data from all projects are stored. He goes through the files looking for a list of risks or problems that occurred during past projects. *I would have been surprised to find one.* To be sure, he asks Tom and the Quality Director and they confirm the result of his research: no historical data on risks from past projects. Then, he opens a blank document, prepares a table with the following headers: No., Title, Description, Probability, Impact, Severity, Cost of Risk, Mitigation plan, Owner. He named it "AlphaProject-RiskRegister", takes his computer and goes to the meeting room where all the people he has invited are waiting for him.

"So, let's go!" he says, in a motivated tone. "Today, we're going to address the risks. But first, we need to agree on what I mean by 'risk'."

"Good idea," a participant adds, "it makes sure we talk about the same thing."

"Exactly!" Alan confirms.

"OK," he continues, "I'll refer to the definition given by a world-known project management professional organization. It's called 'Project Management Institute' or PMI. Moreover, for those interested, it has published a book on methodology, processes and tools on project management, and updates it regularly. This book, known as pmbok, is considered the 'bible of project management' in the project management world. Better, it offers certifications for those who are willing to professionalize in project management."

"Oh, yes? Not bad!" Esin interrupts. "What is their website? I'd like to know more about those certifications."

"Simply pmi.org for the US site and pmi-france.org for France. I really recommend to those who are attracted by project management to take at least one of the certifications. It restructures the brain and can significantly boost your career."

"Me," Gama says jokingly, "the PMI I know in France is 'Protection Maternelle et Infantile' which literally means 'Maternal and Infant Protection'".

A burst of laughter in the room.

"OK," Alan resumes, laughing, "let's go back to our definition of risk. 'A project risk is an uncertain event or condition that, if it occurs, has a positive or negative effect on one or more project objectives such as scope, schedule, cost and quality'".

"Positive effect?" someone asks spontaneously.

"Yes! When the effect is positive, it's called 'opportunity' and when it's negative, it's called 'threat'. It will be clearer later, you'll see!"

"Hum," Gama says. "I can see what you're getting at. When you think about it, it makes sense. We are so used to trying to avoid threats, and we forget that we can also act on opportunities to achieve our desires. Normal! It's our primary survival instinct. But there're also opportunities in our everyday life: you just need to know how to open wide your mind to recognize them and not miss them.

"Absolutely!" Delly adds. "I totally agree with Gama. Sometimes even things that seem like a threat are an opportunity when you dig a little; this happens often to me. I only take a step back, think quickly and by magic, the threat turns into an opportunity. But, for that to work, you must first have in mind a clear objective. That is the starting point!"

The participants comment on Delly's remark and start telling each other about the opportunities they have had in their life.

"OK, OK, OK," Alan says. "Let's go back to our main subject of the moment after this short philosophical digression. The second point of alignment: how to formulate risks?"

He pauses briefly before resuming as if to let the group try to answer.

"It's very simple; all you need is to make sure the following elements appear in its description:"

- ✓ The cause, ie the situation that causes the risk
- ✓ The event, ie the threat or likely opportunity
- ✓ The impact on the project objectives

"Uh ... Can you give an example?" Delly asks, confused.

"Of course!"

Alan goes to the board then writes and reads at the same time: "Delay in receiving the AXM software license that could postpone the start of the management module integration leading to deliver Centragiciel v1 late."

"I let you read and find in this description the cause, the event, and the impact."

He pauses again to give the time to the participants to think.

"OK, I've got it!" Delly says. "So, in your example, the cause is the delay in receiving the license, the event is to postpone the integration of the module 'management', and the impact on the project objectives is the delay of Centragiciel v1 delivery."

"Exactly!"

"Well, this type of delay is also possible for materials we need in the project. So, should we consider them as risks as well?" Delly asks.

"Yes!" Alan responds. "However, the probabilities that they occur might be different or the impacts might not be the same. That's why It's necessary to specify separately the risks per external deliverable. This helps to better follow them. Another example: There's also that difficulty often encountered to obtain clarifications on certain business requirements while they are being developed."

Alan opens his document "AlphaProject-RiskRegister" and notes in the column "Description" as they formulate the risks.

"Of course," he continues, "even if the requirements have been already validated, developers could need business expertise throughout the project for clarification and possible adjustments. For this risk, we can mention: 'Inadequate support of business which can delay the understanding of certain requirements and lead to their redevelopment.'"

"OK, it's clear!" Gama says. "The cause is the lack or insufficiency of business support; the event is the misunderstanding of certain requirements and the impact is to rework what is already done."

"Personally, I can see a technical risk on performance," Esin says. "Given the growing number of the module 'management' users, our servers might be overloaded."

"OK, we're almost there! Let's do it together with a question and answer," Alan suggests.

"What is the cause?"

"The growing number of the module 'management' users," answers Esin.

"What is the potential threat from it?"

"The servers that host Centragiciel may be overloaded with simultaneous connections," Esin says again.

"What will be the impact on the project if that dreaded threat occurs?"

"Users won't be able to access Centragiciel," Gama answers.

"In other words," Esin says, "it gives us something like: 'The growing number of the module 'management' users that could lead to server overload and prevent users to access Centragiciel.'"

"Perfect! I note that too," Alan says.

"But so far, no opportunity has been mentioned; can we really find one on a project like this?" Esin asks.

"I do see one," Zely says: "'Renegotiation of pricing conditions with our provider People2YourC that could lower the current daily rate and reduce the team cost.'"

"Here is another similar," Alan adds: "'Negotiation ongoing to hire an expert that will work on the billing module to make its evolutions and parameterization more efficient.'"

"Yeah, it will be cool if this expert joins us. But, isn't sure he's hired?" Zely asks.

"No… because of the contractual constraints between AssurTGE and the publisher. But there's a one-in-two chance he joins us during the project."

Together they list many risks and very quickly run out of ideas.

"In fact, now that we've understood how to formulate the risks, the most complicated is to identify them, I think," one of the participants in the group says. Any trick for that?"

"OK, here's how we will proceed," Alan responds. "We will play a project 'pre-mortem' game. We'll focus on the 'fishing for threats'".

Alan takes a sip and continues. The group listens religiously, curious to discover the technique he is going to propose.

"You will imagine that you're in the future, the project is completed but failed. You then meet to determine the reasons for the failure. To find these reasons, imagine that you're on the project, each fulfilling his role. Then, again with your imagination, scroll through the project execution from the beginning to the final delivery, even until the moment you received the first user's feedbacks. Proceed step by step, and write down all the events that come to your mind."

He thinks for a moment looking for how to better explain his thought, then repeats:

"Well! Let me say it differently. You are in the future at the end of this failed project. With your imagination, you are visualizing the film of the progress of the project, phase by phase, from beginning to end. Each time, you capture an event that negatively impacts the project scope, its budget, or its deadline, or the quality of what is delivered or all of the above."

"Hold on!" Ethan interrupts him. "By 'phase by phase' you mean 'definition of needs', 'specification', 'design', 'development', etc.?"

"Exactly!"

"Oh yeah ..." Ethan exclaims. "That's right; it must be fun to visualize the project scenes like a movie! But there, we have to get very creative. Anyway, let's try!"

"Yes," Alan says. "Visualize is the key!"

"You each have five minutes to imagine the list of reasons why the project failed," he continues. "Then, in turn, everyone will read an idea from his list and write it on the board. Then, you'll start again the roundtable until exhausting your lists."

"Obviously," another person interrupts him, "we'll likely have a problem with the formulation of the risks, no? We have little time to imagine the ideas. As we aren't experts in risk formulation, it's not going to be short? We will end up wanting to capture ideas quickly and at the same time, formulate them as you ask. I'm afraid it disturbs us and slow us down!"

"You've done well to notice this point," Alan responds. "We will do step by step. Just focus on catching ideas and write them down as you wish. We will formulate the corresponding risks afterward. Of course, this does not prevent those who feel comfortable in formulating the risks of doing it at the same time as they capture their ideas!"

"Can we start? Is that clear?" he asks.

Silence.

"OK," Alan says. "This could help you. What are the areas in which we can encounter problems?"

Participants cite untidily the areas and he writes them down on the board, repeating them aloud. In that way, the group progressively develops the list below. He finishes writing them and immediately goes back to his computer to take notes.

- ✓ Project scope
- ✓ Technology
- ✓ Quality
- ✓ Resources
- ✓ Communication
- ✓ Supplier
- ✓ Dependency between modules
- ✓ Dependence on other projects
- ✓ Stakeholder involvement

"Hmm, what are these categories for?" a participant asks.

"Threats could come from many sources," Zely replies. "Knowing the possible sources will help us find them quickly; they guide us. Is that the idea behind?"

"That's exactly the point!" Alan confirms. "But, be careful! Every time, write down all the ideas that cross your mind without trying to limit yourself to a given category."

"Well, I'm repeating myself again to get you back into it," he continues. "Imagine yourself in the future. The project ended bad! Yes, very bad! It messed up. Centragiciel is delivered several months late. It's unusable! The team is exhausted and only looking for one thing: get out of the project quickly and do not repeat such an experience! In short, let's say it's a disaster. We will start with the category 'project scope'. Try to imagine the events related to the project scope that led to such a failure. Give free rein to your imagination; do not repress any idea that crosses your mind. Think about requirement gathering, definition, specification, development, etc."

"So, can we start?" Alan asks again.

The group agrees. The room is immersed in silence. Alan doesn't speak anymore. After a few minutes, he says: "Remember the rules. In three minutes, everyone will share their ideas with the group." Still a deep silence. After five minutes, he marks the end: "Stop, time is over!" All participants start talking to each other at the same time in a hubbub.

Alan waits a few minutes for the room to be quiet again.

"So, could you come up with ideas? Who wants to share one of his ideas first?" Alan asks.

"It's really hard your exercise," a participant responds. "focused as I might be, I haven't found any idea. In fact, I don't even know where to begin."

All the participants start talking again at the same time, causing even more noise than before. Some say, "Yes, it's the same!" Others "I confirm, really hard!"

"OK… quiet please…" Alan says loudly enough to be heard. "That's normal; it's the beginning. It will be easier afterward by practicing."

Silence.

"Let me give you an example. Suppose we delivered Centragiciel, and users find that more than half of the features they were expecting missed. One can imagine an event having a negative consequence on the scope as: 'The end users are not involved during the gathering of the needs and therefore the functional requirements cover only part of their needs'. There, do you agree that we can say there is a reason for the project failure?"

Some participants say, "Oh, yes, all right," others say, "Well done!" One adds more loudly to be heard by all: "Ah, I agree, if we forget half the work, it's not cool! Failure is certain!"

"Well, here we go. We'll start again with the category 'Scope'. Remember, look no further. Do not repress any idea that crosses your mind, write them down on paper!"

He gives the starting signal. The room is quiet again. Total calm. No participant writes. Alan worries and wonders if they will succeed in finding ideas this time. To occupy the time that seems long, he gets up, walks to the door, opens it quietly to make no noise, takes a look in the hallway as if looking for someone, carefully closes the door and returns to his place. When he returns, all the participants are writing something on their notebook or laptop for some. After five minutes, Alan says, it's time to stop.

Again, discussion among participants for a short while.

"So, is it a little simpler this time? Who shares one of his ideas first?" he asks.

A participant proposes to start, goes to the board, and writes while reading: 'All business areas are not represented during the workshop on definition of need and therefore many necessary and useful features were missing'. Proud of the list of ideas he could find, he was going to move on a second when Alan stops him.

"Great! Thank you," Alan says. "Now, let's continue with the person on your left. We will go around the table. You will take turns until you exhaust your list in the current category."

The next person stands up and mentions: 'The business representatives were not available to see the product intermediate stages while developers were building it to adjust it if necessary.'

Participants exhaust their ideas for the category 'Scope'. Alan suggests they take a short break before continuing with the following areas.

After the break, they continue with the category 'Technique'.

"OK, here we go again. Can you see what could have happened technique-wise on that crazy project?" Alan says.

A developer says, laughing: "Ah ... technique! If they could listen to us ...". Alan also laughs: "This is actually the time to listen to you!"

Five minutes later, a developer suggests: "We discover very late that many SQL commands used in stored procedures are not compatible with our database management system version."

A second says: "We discover very late that the codes of some modules are so complex that it's very difficult or impossible to modify them".

A third adds: "The number of interfaces appears high and made the architecture too complex. So, any modification or correction requires a disproportionate workload."

"Wow! You've found many ideas in this area," Alan says surprised.

"Yes, the machine 'Imagination' is now launched," replies a participant, happy.

"So, let's move on to the next category," Alan says.

The group proceeds that way, category by category and produces a long list which extract is below:

Scope

- ✓ End users are not involved in requirements gathering and therefore the functional requirements only cover part of their needs.
- ✓ All business areas are not represented during the definition of the need and therefore many necessary and useful features were missing from the final product.
- ✓ Business representatives were not available to see the intermediate steps of the product as it was built to adjust it if necessary.
- ✓ Many functional features not required by business are developed at the initiative of the developers.
- ✓ Many non-functional requirements are missed during requirements definition.

Technical

- ✓ We discover very late that many SQL commands used in stored procedures are not compatible with the version of our database management system.
- ✓ We discover very late that the codes of some modules are so complex that it's very difficult or impossible to modify them unless they're completely redeveloped.
- ✓ The number of interfaces appears high and made the architecture too complex. So, any modification or correction requires a disproportionate workload.
- ✓ It was discovered very late that the interface between module X and module Y causes a bottleneck that affects performance.
- ✓ The server that host the sources of some modules crashed whereas there are no recent backups.
- ✓ As delivery approaches, a developer mistakenly removes a class shared by all modules, causing a bug whose cause is very hard to find.

Quality

- ✓ The business representatives are not involved in the validation of the test plan and therefore many use cases cause critical anomalies not detected during the validation but only encountered later in production.
- ✓ We realize very late that Centragiciel overloads quickly in many scenarios of use.
- ✓ A change is made at the last minute and causes regressions that take weeks to fix.
- ✓ A fix considered "minor" is delivered quickly without being validated by the validation team in order to save time and cause a critical anomaly.

Resource

- ✓ Some experts are not available to support the team.
- ✓ Many developers who work on critical activities are often solicited on other projects and therefore are not focused on their activities.
- ✓ Inexperienced developers are positioned on complicated tasks without training on technology and therefore consume a lot of senior developers' time.
- ✓ There is no budget anymore to extend certain contractor's contract on the project.
- ✓ The atmosphere is tense in the team and they make many mistakes or rush through their work.

Provider

- ✓ Late delivery of suppliers (licenses, external software components and hardware).
- ✓ Delay in the development of the internal component CC causing a delay in the delivery of Centragiciel.

Other

- ✓ Many project activities are forgotten and the project time and budget are underestimated.
- ✓ The project manager wrongly estimated a lot of activities and therefore the project time and budget are underestimated.

Alan pauses for a moment, looks around the room and continues:

"Be careful! Do not go so fast on this list. Review it! Take a few minutes to think and see if you have any other risk ideas. It's the basis of the next step of our risk analysis."

12

"Now," Alan begins, "let's come back to the present moment. Get back in our project's context. We will retain the ideas that are really applicable to AlphaProject."

"Oh yes, we must," Alfan adds. "I've really thrown out all the possible bad things that could happen during a project; not sure they're all applicable in our context."

The group goes through the list of ideas together and marks "NA" in front of those he thinks to be too imaginary and cannot apply to AlphaProject. Alan displays only the list of selected ideas.

"OK," Alan resumes, "it's time to deduce the risks. We will reword them together so that they are easy to understand. Do you remember our famous 'Cause / Event / Impact' model?"

"Of course," one participant says, "this is not going to take long, now that we have got the ideas. It's just a matter of rewording."

"Um," Alan says. "For some ideas, that's correct. But we'll probably fall on others where it will be necessary for example to ask the question like: 'why the event could happen?'"

Alan projects on the screen the document "AlphaProject-RiskRegister" that contains the list of risks they had already registered. He keeps open the document that contains the ideas and continues.

"Well, if you take the idea 'end users are not involved in the gathering of needs and therefore the functional requirements only cover part of their needs', the risk can be quickly formulated. Any proposal?"

Alfan starts:

"Something like ...: 'Non-involvement of end users, which may cause an incomplete definition of the need, leading to the redevelopment of Centragiciel.'"

"That's it!"

A participant reacts:

"Uh ... I'd have rather said it another way ... 'Non-involvement of end users, which might cause an incomplete definition of need, leading to rework'."

"Isn't that the same?" another participant replies. "I could turn it to you in many different ways too!"

"Yes, of course, that's okay too!" Alan answers. "The key is to bring out the 'probable causes/event/impacts' and express the risk in a simple way so that it's understood."

Alan gets up, goes to the board, turns to the screen where the list of ideas is displayed and continues.

"But, if you take this one..."

He writes while reading: "We discover very late that many SQL orders used in stored procedures are not compatible with our database management system version."

"It will need a little extra effort to deduce the risk, I think. Someone wants to try?" he asks.

Some participants all together begin laughing: "Well, who has proposed this complicated idea?"

"Don't laugh, guys," one of them intervenes. "We often face this problem! And I've never seen anyone anticipate it. We do well to mention it here."

His colleagues continue laughing and say, "Ah, you are the culprit; we're waiting for your formulation".

Suddenly, Alfan interrupts and turns himself in:

No! He is not! I did propose this idea. In the context of AlphaProject, here is what I meant: "Insufficient knowledge of the specificities of the DBMS in the team which might result in writing incompatible SQL commands leading to redevelop them."

"Perfect!" Alan resumes. "Before we start to take them in the order, let's look at this one: 'We discover very late that the codes of some modules are so complex that it's very difficult or impossible to modify them unless redeveloped completely'. It could give: 'Lack of inspection of legacy codes before the estimate of developments which may result in redeveloping some modules and increase project costs and time'. Couldn't it?"

The team goes through the ideas one after the other. Alan writes the descriptions in the risk register. It's 12:10 am, the risk identification is complete. Alan suggests that participants go to lunch and back at 1:30 pm to continue.

Some go to the canteen to have lunch together. Sitting around a circular table, they tell each other their evening of the day before, their last film and the last book they read. Ethan, staring at his smartphone, burst out laughing and begins to tell his story out loud so that all his colleagues can hear. They listen to him all, calmly.

"According to the scientists," he starts, "two black holes have collided and this would have caused waves in the Universe."

"Hmm ... black hole. What's that, again?" Delly asks.

"These are super-dense celestial objects, or compact ones if you want, that attract and trap any matter or light that passes near them,"

Ethan answers. "They are impressive, even the light can't escape their force of attraction."

All his colleagues listen attentively, eager to know more about the story.

"The two which collided," he continues, "would be eight or fourteen times as great as our star, the Sun. Astronomical numbers, you might say, when you know that we're speaking about billions of billions of billions of tons just for the Sun's mass."

With a very skillful movement, he wraps around his fork a portion of the succulent spaghetti carbonara on his plate, swallows it and accompanies it with a sip of sparkling water.

"Imagine the scene," he continues, accompanying his description with the movements of his hands, focused as if he was watching a movie. "Two huge stars wander in space, each one rotating around each other. Suddenly, they head towards each other at a crazy speed of about 150 000 km / h while continuing to turn one around the other, come closer by describing spirals increasingly tight, and in a split second, boom ... collide! They then merge into a gigantic black hole of about twenty times the sun's mass. Twenty times! Huge! The impact vibrates the whole space as predicted by the physicist Albert Einstein just a century ago. Massive ripples begin to spread in space like waves caused by a stone thrown into a lake."

"Wow!" exclaims one of the colleagues. "It was these waves that were detected on Earth only on September 14, 2015?"

"Exactly," Ethan responds. "They spread to us and could be detected for about a second with sophisticated instruments. Scientists call these ripples gravitational waves. The most surprising thing is that, according to the scientists, this collision occurred 1.4 billion light years from Earth. These waves traveled for more than a billion years before reaching us."

“More than a billion years? Unbelievable!” Delly says. “What a beautiful trip in a so distant past! But hey, we have to finish eating fast and come down to Earth. It's time to get back to work.”

It’s 1:30 pm, the workshop resumes.

“Now, it’s time to analyze our risks,” Alan begins.

“Uh ... Analyze the risks!?” Delly exclaims. “Are you sure we're the right persons for that? I am not sure we know much about it. Well ... not me anyway!”

“You will see,” Alan continues, “this part will be simpler than the definition of the risks. Remember, the events we have described are uncertain. During the course of our project, they could occur but they could also not happen. Right? Well, you have now the privilege to say what the probabilities for them to occur are.”

“A probability to occur?” one of the participants asks. “We must be soothsayer to answer that, no? For example, we will say that the probability of an event A to occur is 60% or the one of an event B is 50%?”

“No,” Alan responds. “The AssurTGE Quality Director has provided us with ranges of probabilities that will help us to define the level of uncertainty of the risks. We will therefore, reason by referring to these ranges; no need to give exact probabilities. Finally ... we are not in an exact science! This makes the work easier.”

Alan opens a document and displays on the screen the table below, whispering, “The probability is measured on a four-level scale.”

Scale	Probability	
4	90 - 99 %	Near certainty
3	50 - 89 %	More likely
2	10 - 49 %	Less likely
1	1 - 9 %	Not likely

Table 1-5. Probability definition

"Do you see?" he continues. "There are scales. I let you read. For example, when we think that the probability of an event to occur is between 1 and 9 %, we will mark the risk as 'Not Likely'. When it's between 90 and 99 %, it will be considered as 'Near Certainty', and so on. Just refer to this table."

"Well, it looks simple!" Delly says. "But why would we consider an event which probability is between 1 and 9 % as 'Not Likely'? We could also say that it's 'Likely', right?"

"Absolutely!" Alan confirms. "In another company, this might be the case. This work of definition of risk scales is already done, discussed and validated by AssurTGE under the Quality Director's control. Now, projects benefit from that to qualify their risks."

He pauses and drinks a sip of water.

"Before I show you another matrix, is it clear to everyone?" he asks.

"Let me check if I've got it right," Delly responds. "I think my risk 'Inadequate support of business experts which can delay understanding of certain requirements and lead to their redevelopment' must be between 50 % and 89 % chance of happening. So, it can be marked as 'More Likely' then?"

"Referring to the matrix, that's exactly the case!" Alan confirms. "And that's what I'm going to write in front of the risk in the 'Probability' column."

"We will do the same for the impact: rate it on a scale," he continues.

Delly smiles and says:

"And the AssurTGE Quality Director has also provided you with a grid for that."

"Absolutely! And, I'm going to display it," Alan confirms.

He scrolls down a little lower in the document he had opened and shows the following table while commenting: "The impact (threat case) is measured on a scale of five levels according to the criteria defined in this matrix: Very low, Low, Moderate, High, and Very High."

Project objectives	Scales				
	Very Low	**Low**	**Moderate**	**High**	**Very High**
Cost	Overcost < 5 %	Overcost 5 % - 10 %	Overcost 10 %-20 %	Overcost 20 %-40 %	Overcost > 40 %
Time	Delay < 5 %	Delay 5 % - 10 %	Delay 10 %-20 %	Delay 20 %-40 %	Delay > 40 %
Scope	Custom labels missing but standard labels displayed	Labels and texts remain understandable by the user	Functional content affected but the result remains coherent (Excluding wording and texts)	Affected functional content giving an inconsistent result	Unusable module
Quality	Only 2 labels are impacted by use case	More than 2 labels impacted by use case	The result does not match the specified functional rules	Incoherent result display	Unusable module

Table 1-6. Definition of Impact Scales (case of thread)

"Here also, it's simple," he says, "I'll let you read the matrix."

He waits a few seconds, asks if the group follows him and resumes:

"We'll qualify an impact as 'Very Low', 'Low', 'Moderate', 'High' or 'Very High'. Now, the question is: When will we say that an impact is 'very Low' or 'Low'? Or takes any other value of this list?"

"Well, it's simple!" Esin responds. "The answer is in the matrix. For example, if the estimated impact is an additional cost between 10 and 20 %, we'll say that it's 'Moderate', if it exceeds 40 %, we'll say that the impact is 'Very high'."

"That's it!" Alan confirms. "But the impact can be something other than an extra cost. Do you remember the risk on the scope? If the impact on the scope is 'Unusable Module', it will be marked as 'Very High'."

"Hum," Esin says. "So, for each risk, it's necessary to evaluate the damage it would cause if it occurred?"

"Yes, exactly!" Alan responds. "And that's why you have to do it as a team with the right people to get as close as possible to a correct qualification."

The group goes through all the risks and discusses their likelihood and impact one after the other. In doing so, they qualify them. Alan fills the 'Probability' and 'Impact' columns of the risk register as the discussion progresses and writes down the extra costs when possible. Noticing that the group is distracted, he proposes a fifteen minute break.

Then, everyone goes about their own business: some make personal phone calls, others consult the messages on their smartphone or emails on their computer. Betty and Esin settle in one of the rest areas near the meeting room.

"I learn every day with my son," Betty says. "He brought me another story last night."

"Aah ... kids ... With the internet and their smartphone, they have more than a library at hand. As long as they make good use of it! So, tell, what did he tell you?" Esin asks.

"In fact, he is more and more interested in Greek mythology and tells us many of his readings at dinner."

"That's excellent, for a boy of twelve."

"Last night, he told me Europe was a Phoenician princess."

"Wait! Wait! Let's start at the beginning so that I follow you. 'Phoenician' would be to say someone from Phoenicia. But where is that?"

"It's a region roughly corresponding to current Lebanon. The Phoenicians are an ancient people from this corner. But well, we're talking about antiquity."

"OK, Europe would be a princess coming from there?"

"Yes, and according to legend, she was approached by Zeus, the supreme god of Greek mythology, and they would have had three children together."

"Oh ... yeah ...! Europe was one of Zeus's conquests then?"

"A real seducer, that Zeus, he had many conquests," Betty adds, bursting into laughter.

"So, our continent Europe is a beautiful princess?"

"Yes, that's what I learned yesterday. Do you have a five or ten-euro bill?"

"Sure, why?" Esin asks, looking surprised.

"Perfect, give me one or the other. Promise, I'll give it back to you."

Esin hands him a folded ten-euro note. Betty takes it and unfolds it. Holding it unfolded with both hands, she raises her arms and presents it in front of Esin's eyes.

"Look, do you see the beautiful Europe's face?" Betty says, smiling.

"Oh yes ... I see the beautiful princess! She's even engraved on our notes! Not bad!"

The break is over, the participants return to their place. The room is quiet and gives the impression that it's the nap time. Alan comes back, smiling.

"Well, guys, I have good news for you," he says. "For today, there's not much left to do. A few crossings of lines and columns and we're done."

All participants start to look at each other. Some are whispering words in their neighbor's ears. Others start laughing as to keep themselves awake.

"In this final stretch of our workshop," he continues, "you'll define now how much each risk is serious, or severe for the project."

"Another odd notion," Esin says.

Another adds, "We should have got right to the point, shouldn't we? Personally, all the risks I mentioned are serious." Alan laughs and says:

"You will follow the same logic as for probabilities and impacts to define the degree of severity of each risk. Some call it 'severity' of risk."

He opens again the document 'quality of AssurTGE', projects it on the screen and goes down until finding the table below:

Impact / Probability	Very High	High	Moderate	Low	Very Low
Near Certainty	Unacceptable	Unacceptable	Critical	Significant	Significant
More Likely	Unacceptable	Critical	Significant	Not significant	Not significant
Less Likely	Unacceptable	Critical	Not insignificant	Not significant	Not significant
Not Likely	Critical	Significant	Not significant	Not significant	Not significant

Table 1-7. Definition of risk severity

One participant says, jokingly, "Ah ... I knew there was still matrix in stock."

"In this case too," continues Alan, "you'll just have to refer to this grid to define the severity of each risk. You recognize the impact on the first line and the probability in the first column. Don't you? Just cross a line and a column and you get the severity. It's deduced simply from the probability and the impact. That's all the work that remains to do today."

"Well, for once, it could have been automated," Ethan says. "No need for a human to do that, it's a job for a machine! For each risk, when you choose the probability and the impact, the 'severity' column should fill automatically. Give me your document, and I'll complete it in two minutes. What is the next step?"

"Well spotted, Ethan!" Alan says, "At the next workshop, we will review the risk response strategies and define action plans for the risks that are 'unacceptable' or 'critical'."

"And, what do we do with the others?" Ethan asks.

"They will be monitored throughout the project," Alan responds. "They will be in a list to watch. We'll talk about it again at the next workshop."

The session ends, all participants return to their office and continue their day's work.

13

It's 11:30 am. The weather is nice and mild outside. Alan opens his window slightly. He hears, faintly far in the distance, the sounds of drums mixed with cheers and shouts of joy from a crowd. *Is this the festival of music in AssurTGE or what? The employees don't care. Is that all they've got to do? Sing, dance and scream in the office while the projects spin out of control.* He decides to get close to understand what's going on. The closer he gets, the more the noise turns into energizing music.

One of the canteens overlooking the courtyard is open to the outside. Flags of a country are displayed everywhere inside and outside the canteen. They're green (vertically on the left), yellow (horizontal at the top) followed by red (horizontal at the bottom). In the courtyard, a group of men and women dressed in traditional African outfits sing and dance. The band plays African drums of different sizes, several types of bells, and many other instruments. A cheerful crowd forming a circle enjoys the show.

Suddenly a mask wearing a conical shape camouflage covered with hay emerges from a corner of the yard while dancing and turning on itself. His hays are dyed in the colors of the flags. The group accelerates the rhythm of the music. The first mask is immediately followed by a second, then a third. The group accelerates the pace by tapping more and more quickly on the bells, singing and dancing at the same time. Women chant lyrics in a foreign language as if to encourage the masks. They dance and run in the center of the circle formed by the spectators. Alan surprises his body moving to the rhythm of the music. *No, not here, you will look ridiculous. Control yourself, Alan*! Moments later, the masks arise. Some insiders remove the camouflage of a mask. There is nothing inside. It's absolutely empty! They put the camouflage back, here we go: the mask starts running and dancing again. The spectators are amazed and cheer. Alan, lost, approaches a young woman.

"Hi! Do you know what's going on?"

"Yes, I am part of the organizers. This is one of the big theme meals that AssurTGE organizes four times a year. The management regularly introduces employees to the cultures of small countries they aren't used to visiting. You must have noticed that the meals in the canteen are not European but rather African."

"Well, I've recognized the flag of the Republic of Benin. So, the dishes are also Beninese?"

"Yes, that's it. Today, we are introducing the culture of this country to our employees. At the same time, this relaxes them."

"I think it's a great idea to escape."

"In fact, the masks are called 'zangbeto'. In the culture of Benin, it seems that it means 'Guardian of the night'. They would be spirits that watch over the inhabitants in the night and chase evil spirits and the thieves."

"Oh yeah? And what will be the next culture to discover?"

"We'll change Continent. It will be another small country in Asia."

Alan's phone alarm rings. After this brief period of escape, he suddenly finds himself even more motivated to resume the course of his day's work: the spirit of 'zangheto' has undoubtedly made its effect. He strides back to his office.

2:30 pm, the workshop begins.

"Yesterday," Alan recalls, "we identified and analyzed risks. We decided to provide responses to the risks that have Severity 'Unacceptable' and 'Critical'. Well, that's what we're going to do now."

"Aaaah," cried one of the participants. "The moment I was waiting for has finally come. It's good to list the risks, but if it's just to look at them, we'll have lost all our time. Of course, we must define how to prevent them."

"Before attacking them one after the other," Alan says, "first, I'll explain the strategies and possible responses that can be made. This will inspire us."

"Wow ... Strategy! Guys, be careful of your brains. Fasten your seatbelt, that's not going to be easy," one participant says.

The room laughs.

"Well, in response to a threat or an opportunity we can ..."

Alan goes to the board and writes, "Avoid the threat or exploit the opportunity".

"This deserves an explanation!" he continues, taking a few steps towards the participants. "Yes, if it's a threat, it can be eliminated outright by simply removing its cause. In the case of an opportunity, we can completely eliminate the uncertainty associated with it."

He stops a few moments to let the group think.

"What do you mean by 'be eliminated outright?'" Alfan asks.

"For example," Alan responds, "as a consequence of the threat, to prevent it from happening, we can decide one of the following actions: remove the part of the project that could cause the risk, remove the resource that could cause risk, extend time, decrease scope, etc."

"Oh yes ...!" Alfan exclaims. "Indeed, by doing so, we can eradicate the threat."

"Exactly!" Alan confirms. "On the other hand, to exploit an opportunity, we can, for example, decide to add resources or reorganize the project which increases the chance of the opportunity to occur."

Alan marks a new break, probably to retain the group's attention.

"OK, it's clear!" Alfan says.

"Another strategy is to 'Transfer the threat or share the opportunity'. In the case of a threat, we'll transfer to a third party all or part of the impact as well as the responsibility of the response."

"Obviously we won't transfer it to just anyone, I guess!" Alfan remarks.

Some participants nod to confirm Alfan's remark.

"Exactly!" Alan responds, "The third party must be able to bear the responsibility of course."

"Ah, that's what we do by taking insurance then?" Alfan asks.

"Well done Alfan! This is a good example of risk transfer. And that's also what we do by outsourcing all or part of something we have to achieve."

"OK, I understand now. But, in the case of outsourcing, don't we also take another risk?"

"Absolutely! That is why we should always do the risk analysis before signing an outsourcing contract. That way, we'll have a good knowledge of the risks induced by outsourcing and take the necessary precautions in the contract."

Participants start whispering something causing a background noise in the room. Alan stops for a moment and asks if they follow his explanations well.

Again, silence in the room. He pursues.

"In the case of an opportunity, it's the same; we give the responsibility to a third party because he is the one who has the necessary expertise to achieve what we want to do. We can for example work in partnership with him or establish any other form of collaboration but he is the one who is responsible for the response, not us."

He scans the whole room.

"Let's move on to another strategy."

"Ah, there're still other possibilities?" Alfan asks.

"Yes! Mitigate the threat or improve the opportunity. This one is very simple. For a threat, you only need to **lower** to an acceptable threshold, its probability or its impact or both at the same time. Depending on the threat, we can imagine for example to perform more tests, or make a prototype to validate a concept before going further, recruit a resource to reduce the unavailability of resources on a given expertise, etc."

"And on the other hand," he continues, "for an opportunity, by symmetry to the strategy applied to a threat, you'll just need to ..."

"Wait, wait" Gama interrupts. "Let me guess. It must be: '**increase** the probability or the impact or both at once!'".

"Great!" Alan cries. "In this case, for example, a more experienced resource can be assigned to an activity to reduce the time it takes to complete; we can take actions to increase the chance of hiring an expert, or to increase the chances of a negotiation of an expert's daily rate, etc."

Alan looks back at the other participants to try to read from their faces if they understood his explanations.

"Be careful! You must all understand the possible strategies before moving on. So far, do they seem clear to you? If not stop me, take a few moments to think about each of them."

Some answer "clear!" Others "perfect!" And others "crystal clear!"

"But, what do we do if we can't apply any of these strategies for one reason or another?" Gama asks.

"Good question," Alan replies. "This leads us straight to the last possibility: Accept the threat and the opportunity. With this strategy, whether for a threat or an opportunity, we decide to take no action until the risk occurs. However, often, a contingency plan is defined and will be followed if the risk occurs."

"Wow!" Gama exclaims. "Four response strategies. Let me recapitulate those of a threat, without looking at the board to see if I've caught everything."

"Good idea, to repeat them aloud will serve everyone," Alan says.

"Well, I recall them:"

- ✓ Avoid the risk by defining actions to eliminate it entirely. It can be for example: remove the part of the project or the resource likely to cause the risk, extend the time, reduce the scope, etc.
- ✓ Transfer the impact and the responsibility of the response to a third party; as we do when we insure ourselves against a risk.
- ✓ Mitigate it by lowering its probability or impact to an acceptable threshold or both. For example, by performing more tests, or validating a concept with a prototype, etc.
- ✓ Simply accept the risk by not taking any action until it occurs. Define a contingency plan to apply in case the risk occurs.

"You have a good memory!" Alan says, happy. "Excellent! Does anyone else want to do the same for an opportunity?"

The hubbub in the room.

"Yes, I do! I'll try," Delly says.

Silence.

"Okay, let's do it:"

- ✓ Exploit the opportunity by removing the cause of its uncertainty. For example: add resources or reorganize the project outright.
- ✓ Share with a third party the impact and the responsibility for the response. For example, we develop a partnership with a specialized third party that will achieve our work.
- ✓ Enhance the opportunity by increasing its probability or impact or both. For example, assigning a more experienced resource to an activity to complete before the scheduled end date.
- ✓ And as for a threat, simply accept the opportunity by not taking any action until the event occurs.

"Wow! You're as good as me," Gama laughs.

All the other participants burst out laughing. They comment on those strategies in a hubbub for a few moments. Alan looks at them, silent, happy to have passed his message.

"I think that deserves a break, doesn't it?" says a voice from the back of the room. "What do you think?"

Thus, the group decides on a quarter of an hour break.

As usual, Betty and Esin spend the time together. It was a nice sunny day outside, they sit in the garden.

"This weekend," Betty says, "I wandered around 'Les Champs Élysée' at night with a friend from New York visiting Paris."

"What did you do with your children?" Esin asks.

"I'm lucky for that, my parents keep them with pleasure when I need it. 'Les Champs Élysée' is beautiful, especially at night. By the way, do you know what I learned?"

"Ah ... your son again, the Greek!" Esin interrupts, laughing.

"Yes, well spotted!" Betty continues, laughing. "In Greek mythology, 'Champs Élysée' would be a part of Greek underworld where virtuous souls lived after death."

"Underworld?"

"Yes, the underworld, that is to say, the abode of the dead, all the dead without exception: the blessed, the unfortunate, and even the souls judged neither good nor bad!"

"Really?"

"Absolutely! And, the place where it was good to live, and where the blessed stayed was called 'Champs Elysées'."

"So, what's about the unfortunate people?"

"Direct to Tartarus! Yes, they were placed separately in a dark place. However, beware. In mythology, the 'unfortunate' are punished criminals! And not people who are unlucky or not happy as we could understand in our everyday language."

"Sure, I see. Can you imagine? To be punished after death simply because one was unlucky during one's life? It would be a double punishment!"

"That's not all. It seems that the Greeks have even reserved a separate place for souls who have accomplished nothing in their lifetime and have led a meaningless life."

"Oh, yeah?" Esin says, surprised, bursting into laughter. "So We'd better accomplish something in our lifetime then? Otherwise, we won't land at 'Champs Elysées'? Well, I'm not going to die wondering, I've learned something new today: Champs Elysées was a sweet place to live in the Greek underworld. So, I'll go there more often now ... in case I don't land there after my death because I'm still looking for what to accomplish in my lifetime."

"Hum ... 'accomplish' ... It makes me think suddenly. Leave something useful to future generations, and contribute to the endless chain of improving living conditions for humanity. That was a good point from the Greeks!"

14

It's the end of the break, the workshop resumes.

"Ok," Alan begins, "the types of strategies are now clear. So they'll guide you to define our risk's responses. We'll proceed risk by risk."

"When you look at these strategies well," Alfan says, "it seems that most of the risks will only need to be mitigated. I'm talking about threats of course."

"Exactly!" Alan says, "especially since I've already explored the 'avoid', 'transfer' and 'accept' strategies. In fact, that's often the case."

Alan projects the risk register on the board. He scrolls through it, stops at a risk and reads it aloud:

"'Delay in receiving the AXM software license that could postpone the start of the management module integration leading to deliver Centragiciel v1 late.' How can we mitigate this? So, who wants to start?"

Silence. Nobody is answering. Alan thinks a few seconds and proposes the following action to initiate the movement.

"A solution is to order the licenses well in advance. This will reduce the likelihood of being delivered late."

"Yeah, that's clear, we do it early," Zely says.

"Indeed, this is already a first precaution. Another idea?" Alan asks.

"In fact," says a participant, "it takes a lot of work for suppliers to prepare these types of license. The preparation process is long. That's why delivery takes weeks or sometimes months. So, I think we have to agree with the supplier on milestones and check the progress of the license preparation."

"OK," Alan resumes, "I add: 'Agree with the supplier on milestones to check the progress of the license preparation'".

"These two actions are fine," Alan says. "But I'd add a third: 'In our contract with the supplier, include a penalty clause which provides compensation in case of delay of delivery'. This will reduce, or perhaps even cancel, the compensation we'll have to pay to our internal client if we deliver late."

"In summary, to mitigate this risk, we retain the following three actions:"

He reads aloud to the group: "

- ✓ Order licenses early enough.
- ✓ Agree with the supplier on milestones to check the progress of license preparation.
- ✓ In our contract with the supplier, include a penalty clause that provides compensation if we deliver late."

"Any comments?" Alan asks.

Silence.

"Perfect! Let's move on to the next," he continues.

He moves the cursor on the risk 'Inadequate support of business which can delay the understanding of certain requirements and lead to their redevelopment'.

Diane, a business representative, reacts immediately:

"For this one," I confirm, "given the work to be done, we may have a real concern for availability. I talked about it to my boss. To mitigate the risk, we will recruit an assistant for the project period; it costs 25 k €. It will help us on some of our activities, which will relieve us a bit from some works."

"OK, I write: 'Recruit an assistant to help business and increase their availability," Alan says.

He scrolls his cursor and stops on the risk 'Insufficient support from experts to developers that can delay the understanding of certain technical requirements leading to redevelop them'.

"Well, also here, we just have to hire a technical expert to assist our colleagues," Diane says.

"In the case of technical expertise," explains Alfan, "it's a bit more complicated. For all our activities, we need technical skills and a very good knowledge of our business. And it's hard to find. So, even if we had the finance, this solution wouldn't be applicable."

All participants think. Nobody talks, it's total silence for about a minute. Then, Alfan continues:

"So, I propose to plan in advance complex activities that require technical support. And to share as soon as possible technical deliverables with experts to gather their comments as soon as possible."

"OK perfect, we can also agree with them on milestones to address those technical aspects," adds Alan.

"It's also necessary to share these milestones with their line managers so that they take them into account in their overall planning," a technical representative adds.

"OK, let's summarize," Alan says: "

- ✓ Plan ahead for complex activities that require technical support.

- ✓ Share technical deliverables as soon as possible with the experts to gather their comments as soon as possible.
- ✓ Agree with experts on milestones to address technical issues.
- ✓ Share milestones with the experts' line managers"

"Any remark?" Alan asks.

He waits a few moments and displays the following risk: 'Insufficient knowledge of the specificities of the DBMS in the team which might result in writing incompatible SQL commands leading to redevelop them'.

"I discussed it with my boss and the database guys," Esin says. "We can suggest a two-day training on the specificities of our DBMS. It costs 20 k €. Compared to the time it will help us save, no problem to justify this budget!"

Alan writes: 'Plan a two-day training on the specificities of the DBMS.'

"OK, the next is," Alan says: "'Lack of inspection of legacy codes before the estimate of developments which may result in redeveloping some modules and increase project costs and time'".

"I'll save you the time!" Alfan says. "It's necessary to conduct technical studies of the existing codes before estimating the workload and share the results with the teams."

"And," Alan adds, "include the developers who participated in these studies in the workload estimates workshop."

"Perfect," Alan says, "so to summarize:"

- ✓ Conduct technical studies of the existing codes before estimating the workload and share the results with the teams
- ✓ Involve in the workload estimates workshop developers who participated in the codes studies.

The group defines the risks responses. Alan updates the 'Mitigation Plan' and 'Probability' columns in the Risk Register (see Section 3, Table 3.6) as they progress.

"Wait two seconds Alan," interrupts Delly, "how do you get the values in the column 'Cost of risk?'"

"Ah ... Yes, I didn't explain it. It's simply the probability multiplied by the financial impact, I mean the extra cost. The sum of this column will give me the amount of the budget of the provisions to cover the residual risks (see an example of calculation in Appendix 6, table 2.15) in other words those which will remain after our risk analysis.

"OK," Delly says, "but no matter how well we predict everything, there will always be risks that will have completely escaped us. Right? There may be some unexpected events, no?"

"Absolutely! For these unforeseen events, I'll discuss with Christophe and he will reserve a proportion of the budget to cover them; maybe 5% of the total budget, we'll see. It's not part of my monitoring scope."

The workshop ends and they get a table which extract is below:

Description	Action plan
Delay in receiving the AXM software license that could postpone the start of the management module integration leading to deliver Centragiciel v1 late.	✓ Order licenses early enough. ✓ Agree with the supplier on milestones to check the progress of license preparation. ✓ In our contract with the supplier, include a penalty clause that provides compensation if we deliver late."
Inadequate support of business which can delay the understanding of certain requirements and lead to their redevelopment.	Recruit an assistant to help business and increase their availability.
Insufficient support from experts to developers that can delay the understanding of certain technical requirements leading to redevelop them.	✓ Plan ahead for complex activities that require technical support. ✓ Share technical deliverables as soon as possible with the experts to gather their comments as soon as possible. ✓ Agree with experts on milestones to address technical issues. ✓ Share milestones with the experts' line managers

Table 1-8. Risk responses (Part 1)

Description	Action plan
Insufficient knowledge of the specificities of the DBMS in the team which might result in writing incompatible SQL commands leading to redevelop them.	Plan a two-day training on the specificities of the DBMS.
Lack of inspection of legacy codes before the estimate of developments which may result in redeveloping some modules and increase project costs and time.	✓ Conduct technical studies of the existing codes before estimating the workload and share the results with the teams. ✓ Involve in the workload estimates workshop developers who participated in the codes studies. ✓
The growing number of the module 'management' users that could lead to server overload and prevent users to access Centragiciel.	✓ Refine the requirement on the number of users. ✓ Perform performance tests taking into account the maximum number of users.

Table 1-8. Risk responses (Part 2)

Alan suggests that the group chooses an owner for each risk. He fills the risk register column 'Owner' as the discussions proceed.

"Thanks all, you did a great teamwork," he says. "First, you've identified our project's risks. Then you analyzed them. Finally, you have provided preventative responses to those who need it. Well, our workshop on risk ends at this stage."

He drinks a sip of water and continues.

"As you can imagine, we will implement these preventive actions throughout the project. In addition, every week, we'll re-evaluate all risks and identify new ones. Do you see? A real risk monitoring work still lies ahead of us."

Alfan, proud of the work accomplished, also probably happy that the workshop ends, gets up, fist raised and chants: "Yeah ... the risk fishing has just started!" All his other colleagues follow him and respond all together: "and it will last the whole project lifetime!"

Alan bursts out laughing and exclaims, "Wow, you're very enthusiastic!"

That concludes the meeting. The whole group gets around the coffee machine, discusses a moment, and progressively disperses.

Alan returns to his office and integrates all the risk responses action plans into his initial schedule. To address the residual risks, he calculates the budget and deadline provisions: in worse cases where all risks occur (worst-case scenario) and cases where none of the risks are revealed (best-case scenario). He applies both assumptions to his schedule and thus determines the interval in which the budget and the delivery date vary. He finalizes the project management plan by describing how the project would proceed (see Appendix 6). He attaches it to the email below and sends invitations to business managers, developers group leaders, team leaders, test managers, and production managers to review and validate it together during a working session.

Dear All,

I have grouped in the document AlphaProjectPMP.doc how we will proceed during the rest of the project. It will serve us as a reference for the project execution. For the most part, this is what we have already started practicing together. However, it covers how the project will evolve until the end, not just the first package.

That is why I want us to review it and validate it together in a session. Obviously, we can adjust it during the project when necessary.

To prepare the workshop, I have initiated a Question and Answer document. Thank you to mention your questions. We have a week to complete this 'Questions and Answers' step.

PS: all documents are up to date in the project folder.

Regards,

Alan

The following days, he receives some questions and refines the document as he responds. Most of the time, he gives some details to some parts and completes others.

The day of the meeting, the group reviews together each part, makes the last modifications, agrees on the content and validates the final version.

He extracts the parts such as the project scope, milestones, risks, quality and budget to prepare the presentation to the steering committee. During the project weekly meeting, he presents it to his team and together they make some changes.

A few days later, he presents the plan in Steering Committee meeting. The members validate most of the points presented and request some adjustments on quality monitoring.

Back in his office, he makes the changes requested in the document AlphaProjectPMP.doc and publishes it for information to all those who validated it.

He schedules a kick-off meeting to communicate more widely about the new plan. To this end, he sends invitations to developers, testers, people from maintenance and production teams and branch managers. He asks the directors to forward the invitation to all other people in their subsidiaries who may be involved in the project.

To prepare for the meeting, he takes the document he presented at Steering Committee meeting and adds some information that might interest a wider audience.

It's the kickoff meeting day. All guests are present. Half an hour before the scheduled starting time at 3 pm, they are gathered in the largest hall of the South-East building. There are food and drink in every corner of the room. Christophe was absent as he was traveling for an urgent meeting with the Globalinrance president's team. Tom thanks all the guests and very briefly introduces the session. Alan continues. He introduces to the audience the new direction that the project is heading and answers all their questions. At the end of the session, many people remain in the room and discuss around the delicious cakes arranged throughout the room. It's the end of the day, the room progressively empties.

The next day, Alan and Tom meet at the cafeteria.

"I feel that now the project can only go well," Tom says. "You've even already prepared the tools to follow it. There's nothing more to fear, or nothing more to do except follow the plan."

"Your feeling is correct! However, as the Polish American philosopher and scientist Alfred Korzybski wrote, 'The map is not the territory'. I like this proverb! Of course, we have planned what we can, but there will be problems along the way, surprises and deviations. We'll need to provide solutions to each of these problems, control the project plan execution and adjust it until we meet the objectives set".

Section 2: Project documents

Annex 1 - Project Charter

Annex 2 - Stakeholder Register (extract)

Annex 3 - Stakeholder Analysis Matrix (extract)

Annex 4 - WBS (Work Breakdown Structure)

Annex 5 - WBS Dictionary

Annex 6 - Project Management Plan

Annex 7 - Requirements Traceability Matrix

Annex 1 - Project Charter

Project Title and Description: AlphaProject, Merge of AssurTGE's Information System.

As part of a program designed to standardize Globalinrance group information system, the company AssurTGE launches the project "AlphaProject" that will provide a new centralized management software package called "Centragiciel". This software will help to manage the flow of information between all subsidiaries.

The goal of this project is to design, create and deploy the software.

Project Justification

The project is set up to increase employee's productivity and to centralize the management of all subsidiaries' activities at the European level. The use of a common tool will reduce maintenance costs for at least 500 K€ per year.

Project objectives

The goal of this project is to reduce by 30 % the maintenance costs of the softwares used in the 27 subsidiaries and to increase employee's productivity. The new software will have to double its interface with modern tools of market finance to provide relevant financial information and allow Management to make efficient decisions. Subsidiaries with a network of more than 40 agencies will be deployed in priority. Time is a high priority. Quality, Costs and scope are a medium priority.

- ✓ Time: the deployment of the first subsidiary is expected for March 2023, the last for March 2027 at the latest.
- ✓ Budget: 120 million euros over four years

Project Manager and Authority Level

Alan Sapin is the project manager. He has the authority to select the project team members and determine the final budget.

Resources Preassigned

The entire R & D department is assigned to this project. J.Cabres and D.Yanis are dedicated to the project for their business expertise. The attached file gives the list of 93 people in subsidiaries dedicated to the project for their mastery of existing tools. We will work in partnership with our English software editor and integrator "IntegriPros". Documentation, meetings and communication will be done in English. The project manager will determine other resources needed for the good execution of the project.

Stakeholders

The document "*StakeholderRegister.doc*" in attachment gives the list of stakeholders that the project can impact. This list covers subsidiaries directors, the key users, the heads of AssurTGE's departments and their teams. The subsidiaries departments' managers and their team are available to assist the project manager when necessary.

Stakeholders Requirements As Known

A high-level software specification is attached to this document. Detailed functional requirements, technical requirements such as the expected performance, the high availability and other system requirements will be specified during the project lifecycle. The software must be configurable enough to respond to each country's specificities. To make it easier to use, the software must reproduce some specific features of the systems currently used in each subsidiary. The graphical charter must be configurable to reflect the particularities of each country. These particularities will be identified during the project. The merging of e-commerce and e-mobile management systems is not part of this project.

Deliverables

- ✓ The development plan of the "Core System"
- ✓ The final version of the "Core System"
- ✓ The deployment plan of the "Core System" on the pilot site and its stabilization
- ✓ The transition plan of the migration from current tools to the new version
- ✓ The deployment plan of the 27 subsidiaries with its adaptation per subsidiary

Project Approval Requirements

Deliverables to approve include:

- ✓ The final version of the "Core System"
- ✓ Deployment plan of the "Core System"
- ✓ Transition plan of the migration to Centragiciel
- ✓ Deployment plan of the 27 subsidiaries

The final approval of the project will be made by the Quality Director based on the User Acceptance team's test report.

High-Level Project Risks

- ✓ The need to consider the specificities of each country can reduce the benefits expected from a common software.
- ✓ The cultural diversity of the country can strengthen a strong resistance to the change and lead to a rejection of the tool.

Project Sponsor

Christophe Proudy, President of AssurTGE.

Annex 2 - Stakeholder Register

Name	Title	Site	Contact	Role in Project	Expectations	Interests	Influence	Classification
C.Proudy	President	BE	-	Sponsor	Subsidiary's Satisfaction	High	High	Support
A.Sapin	Consultant	BE	02279 22XX	Project Manager	Project Success	High	Moderate	Support
T.Troyas	CEO	BE	02279 22XX	Program Manager	Project back on track	High	Moderate	Indifferent
D.Legres	Marketing Manager	BE	02279 22XX	Subsidiaries Coordinator	No impact when changing the tool for users	High	High	Support
F.Dros	Customers Manager	BE	02279 22XX	Subsidiaries Coordinator	Reduce his team workload	High	Low	Support
C.Blois	R & D Manager	BE	02279 22XX	Resources Manager	Process improvment	Moderate	Low	Indifferent
Y.Tchin	Quality Manager	BE	02279 22XX	Quality Manager	Process improvment	High	Low	Indifferent
J.Grecos	Subsidiary Director	EN	0182451 XX	EN Resources Manager	Efficient resources use	Moderate	High	Indifferent
P.Brown	Subsidiary Director	FR	0582451 XX	FR Resources Manager	Agility of AssurTGE Support after deployment of the new tool	Moderate	High	Against

Table 2 1. Stakeholder Register (extract)

Annex 3 - Stakeholder Analysis Matrix (extract)

Stakeholder	Interests and Influence	Impact Level	Strategies for gaining support or reducing obstacles
Business managers group A	High interest, high Influence (have identified many potential risks), project support	High	Involve this group in the periodic risk review.
Business managers group B	Moderate interest, high Influence (source of many requirements), difficult to work with	Moderate	✓ Pay attention to the clarity of the requirements. ✓ Do a regular report.
Other managers (Technical & Business)	Moderate interest, high influence (motivated to work on several activities), project support	Moderate	Include them officially in the project management team.
Project team member	Moderate interest, little uncomfortable with his tasks, nervous	Moderate	Schedule training if necessary.
President AssurTGE	High interest, High influence	High	Inform regularly on the progress and purpose.
Subsidiary directors group A	Moderate Interest, High Influence, against the project	High (could influence to stop the project)	Understand the reasons against the project and develop a plan to manage this group based on those reasons.
Subsidiary directors group B	High interest, moderate Influence, Indifferent	Moderate	Keep informed on the progress.
Etc.			

Table 2 2. Stakeholder Analysis Matrix (extract)

Annex 4 - WBS (Work Breakdown Structure)

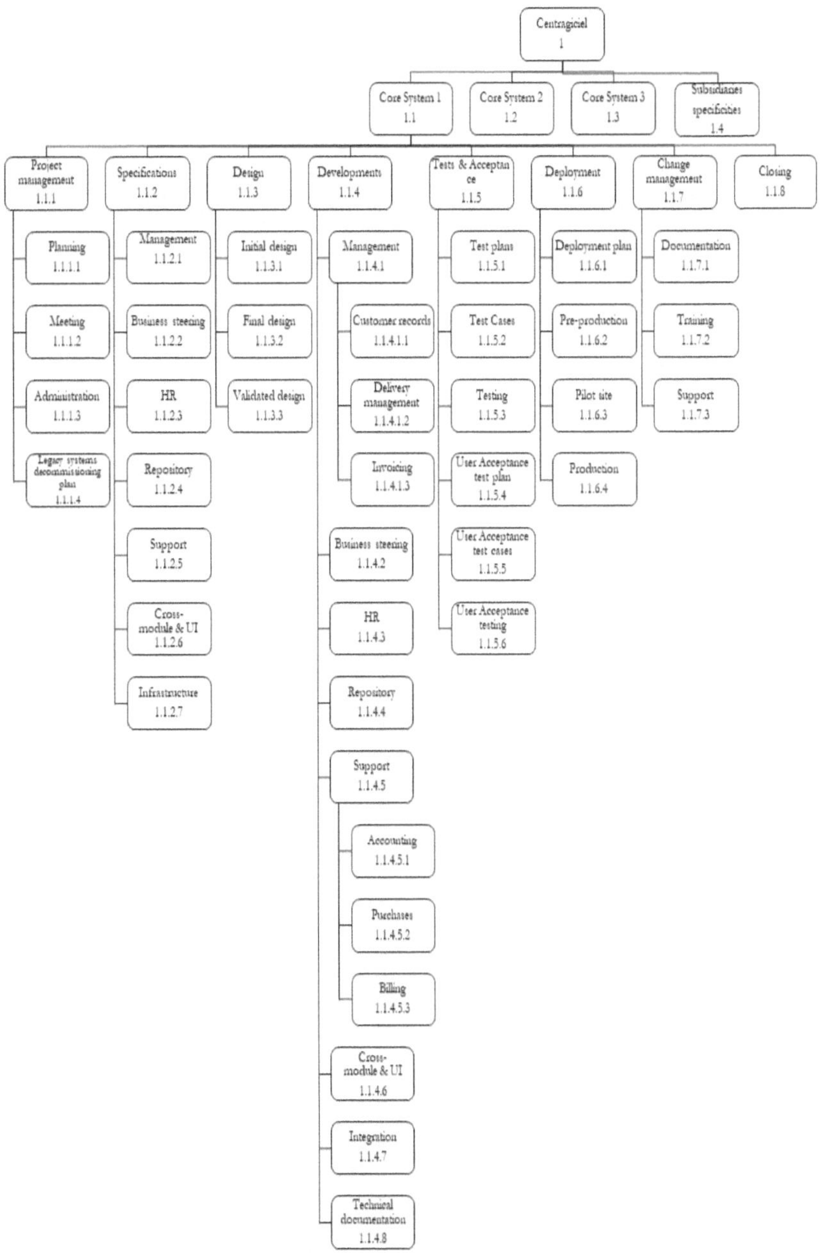

Figure 2.1. WBS (Work Breakdown Structure)

Annex 5 – WBS Dictionary

Level	WBS code	Name of the element	Description	Cost control no.	Manager
1	1	Centragiciel	The software package used by the subsidiaries. It is composed of a group of features common to all the subsidiaries grouped in a "Core System" and features specific to each subsidiary. The "Core System" will be delivered in production incrementally in 3 releases. The subsidiaries specificities will be deployed last.	2	
2	1.1	Core System 1	The first release of the "Core System" to deploy in production for users. It covers the first group of features common to all subsidiaries.	2	
3	1.1.1	Project management	Activities related to project management.	2	Project Manager
4	1.1.1.1	Planning	Activities related to planning. Elaboration of the Project Management Plan and its update.	2	Project Manager
4	1.1.1.2	Meeting	The organization, preparation, animation, and publication of the meetings minutes related to the project.	2	Project Manager
4	1.1.1.3	Administration	All other administrative activities related to the project.	2	Project Manager
4	1.1.1.4	Legacy systems decommissioning plan	Elaboration of a plan that explains the withdrawal strategy of the software currently used by the subsidiaries.		Project Manager

Level	WBS code	Name of the element	Description	Cost control no.	Manager
3	1.1.2	Specifications	Specification of the business features covered by the software package.		Business Managers
4	1.1.2.1	Management	Specification of the modules "Customer records", "Delivery management" and "Invoicing".		
4	1.1.2.2	Business Steering	Specification of the module "Business steering".		
4	1.1.2.3	HR	Specification of the module "Human Resources" features.		
4	1.1.2.4	Repository	Specifications of the modules "Data Repository", "People", "Structure", "Business Process", "Rules".		
4	1.1.2.5	Support	Specifications of the modules "Accounting", "Purchases" and "Billing".		
4	1.1.2.6	Cross-module & UI	Specification of the user interface and the requirements common to all modules.		
4	1.1.2.7	Infrastructure	Specification of the requirements related to the system hosting and the operating.		Production & Operati ons Manager
3	1.1.3	Design	Elaboration of the detailed technical specifications.		Developm ent group leaders

Level	WBS code	Name of the element	Description	Cost control no.	Manager
4	1.1.3.1	Initial design	The first version of the "Core System" detailed specifications.		
4	1.1.3.2	Final design	Last version of the technical specifications. It integrates the remarks of all contributors.		
4	1.1.3.3	Validated design	Validated technical specifications.		
3	1.1.4	Developments	Development and configuration.		
4	1.1.4.1	Management	Development of the modules "Customer records", "Delivery management" and "Invoicing".		
5	1.1.4.1.1	Customer records	Development of the module "Customer records".		
5	1.1.4.1.2	Delivery management	Development of the module "Delivery management".		
5	1.1.4.1.3	Invoicing	Development of the module "Invoicing".		
4	1.1.4.2	Business steering	Development of the module "Business steering".		
4	1.1.4.3	HR	Development of the module "Human Resource".		
4	1.1.4.4	Repository	Development of the modules "Data Repository", "People", "Structure", "Business Process", "Rules".		
4	1.1.4.5	Support	Development of the modules "Accounting", "Purchases" and "Billing".		

Level	WBS code	Name of the element	Description	Cost control no.	Manager
5	1.1.4.5.1	Accounting	Development of the module "Accounting".		
5	1.1.4.5.2	Purchases	Development of the module "Purchases".		
5	1.1.4.5.3	Billing	Development of the module "Billing".		
4	1.1.4.6	Cross-module & UI	Development of the user interface and the requirements common to all modules.		
4	1.1.4.7	Integration	Integration of all modules.		
4	1.1.4.8	Technical documentation	Elaboration of the technical documents of "Core System 1" and the installation documents.		
3	1.1.5	Tests & Acceptance	System Testing & User Acceptance.		
4	1.1.5.1	Test plans	Elaboration of the technical and functional test plans.		System test manager
4	1.1.5.2	Test Cases	Elaboration of the technical and functional test cases. Preparation of data for the tests.		System test manager
4	1.1.5.3	Testing	Technical and functional tests execution.		System test manager
4	1.1.5.4	User Acceptance test plan	Elaboration of the user acceptance test plan.		UAT manager
4	1.1.5.5	User Acceptance test cases	Elaboration of the user acceptance test cases.		UAT manager

Level	WBS code	Name of the element	Description	Cost control no.	Manager
4	1.1.5.6	User Acceptance testing	User Acceptance tests execution.		UAT manager
3	1.1.6	Deployment	Deployment of "Core System 1".		Deployment manager
4	1.1.6.1	Deployment plan	Elaboration of a plan that details the deployment activities in the subsidiaries.		
4	1.1.6.2	Pre-production	Deployment in the environment of pre-production in accordance with the deployment plan.		
4	1.1.6.3	Pilot site	Deployment in production only for the subsidiary chosen as a pilot.		
4	1.1.6.4	Production	Deployment in production for all subsidiaries.		
3	1.1.7	Change management	Change management.		Change management manager
4	1.1.7.1	Documentation	Documentation (booklets, DVD demonstration, training materials).		
4	1.1.7.2	Training	Organization and animation of the users training.		
4	1.1.7.3	Support	Support and help for users.		
1	1.1.8	Closing	Activities that close the development of "Core System 1": update of documents, final lessons learned, balance sheet.		Groups managers

Level	WBS code	Name of the element	Description	Cost control no.	Manager
2	1.2	Core System 2	The second release of the "Core System" to deploy in production for users. It covers the second group of features common to all subsidiaries.		Project Manager
2	1.3	Core System 3	Third and final release of "Core System" to deploy in production for users. It covers all of the remaining features common to the subsidiaries.		Project Manager
2	1.4	Subsidiaries specificities	Specificities of each subsidiary. It covers the specific features of each subsidiary.		Project Manager

Table 2.3 WBS Dictionary

Annex 6 – Project Management Plan

1 Introduction

1.1 Purpose of document

This document is AlphaProject's management plan. It explains how to plan AlphaProject's activities, execute and monitor them until the project closure. At the end of the delivery of each version of the software, the project manager will have to organize a review of the processes described in this document and improve them if necessary.

1.2 Context

As part of a program designed to standardize Globalinrance group information system, AssurTGE launches the project "AlphaProject" that will provide a new centralized management software package called "Centragiciel". This software will help to manage the flow of information between all subsidiaries.

The goal of this project is to design, create and deploy the software.

1.3 Project Life Cycle

The project will follow the life cycle represented by a succession of phases as shown below:

Specification > Design > Developments/Configuration > System Testing > User Acceptance Testing > Deployment > Change management > Closing.

Each phase of the cycle is detailed in the project management handbook available on the intranet at the address "intranet/projects/memento". This paragraph gives an overview.

The cycle must be applied to each of the defined group of requirements, also called release in this document (Core System 1, Core System 2, etc.)

Specification

This phase is devoted to the specification of the requirements documents and the details of Centragiciel's functionalities. At the end of this phase, the requirements documents and the general functional specifications of the "release" must have been produced, the customizations required identified, the adaptations needed by subsidiaries specified.

The elaboration of these deliverables will be done in workshops according to the process below:

1. Prioritize business processes
2. Define the level of detail sufficient to start the overall design
3. By following the order of priority defined in step 1, for each business process,
   - ✓ Define functional and non-functional requirements (see § 4. Requirements Management Plan)
   - ✓ Specify the functionalities covered according to the level of detail defined in step 2 (see § 5. Scope Management Plan)
4. After a series of workshops, when one or more functional areas are covered,
   - ✓ Consolidate and review the requirements for the release
   - ✓ Validate the requirements documents in a workshop
   - ✓ Consolidate and review the general functional specifications of the release
   - ✓ Validate the general functional specifications in a workshop
   - ✓ Decide whether to move to the general design phase (based on criteria defined in step 2)

This phase must be performed for all of the business processes covered by a "release" (but not all the project releases) before moving on to the design.

Design

The key inputs are the requirements document and the general specifications of the release.

During this phase, the general specifications are detailed, the management rules are detailed, the sequence of screens is defined, the interfaces with the other systems are defined and the technical details are specified.

The outputs are the functional architecture document, the technical architecture document and the detailed technical specifications. The details must be sufficient to allow starting the "Developments / Configuration" phase.

Developments / Configuration

This phase consists of developing, configuring and documenting the defined functionalities by following the design documents.

System Testing

The tests of the new functionalities, the regressions testing and the performance & scalability testing will be carried out by the validation teams.

User Acceptance Testing

Acceptance tests and pre-production checks are performed by users prior to deployment in production.

Deployment

After the user's verification in the pre-production environment, the final application is installed on the production servers.

Change management

This phase will take place throughout the project life cycle. User representatives will be involved in the activities of the definition of needs, design and test plans. Prior to production, all users shall be trained in the use of the application. Several training sessions in small groups will be scheduled. Tutorials, documents and videos will be provided to accompany them. During the first week following the deployment in production, groups of the support team will be present physically in the subsidiaries. A strong support will be provided to users for at least 3 months after the deployment.

Closing

The "release" is completed only when all activities in the WBS (Work Breakdown Structure) have been completed and all documentation archived.

1.4 Project Sponsor

The sponsor of this project is Christophe Proudy, President of AssurTGE.

1.5 Project Manager

Allan Sapin is the project manager. He has the authority and responsibility to manage this project in accordance with this Project Plan.

1.6 Project team

The project team consists of people working on at least one of the phases defined in the project lifecycle. The implementation teams are organized in working groups so that they can work in parallel on several modules. The organization chart of the project team and the directory are available on the SharePoint in the project folder at "/SharePoint/Alphaproject."

1.7 Key Stakeholders

The document "CTGCIEL-StakeholdersRegister" on the project sharePoint gives the list of 178 stakeholders that the project may impact. This list includes: subsidiary directors, key users, and AssurTGE department and line managers.

2 Baseline

This paragraph summarizes the scope, schedule and cost baselines.

2.1 Scope baseline

2.1.1 Scope Statement

2.1.1.1 Detailed description of the software content

The software will help subsidiary agencies to manage customer requests, drive day-to-day operations, manage human resources, update customer and prospect repositories, and performed accounting and financial operations. It will also allow AssurTGE to monitor the subsidiaries activities. The features of the first release are detailed in the documents "AP-DetailedSpecifications" in the project folder on the SharePoint.

2.1.1.2 Project deliverables

Below is the list of main deliverables expected:

- ✓ The development plan of the "Core System"
- ✓ The final version of each increment of the "Core System"
- ✓ Deployment plan of the "Core System" on pilot site and its stabilization
- ✓ Transition plan from legacy tools to Centragiciel
- ✓ Deployment plan of 27 countries with adaptations per subsidiary

2.1.1.3 Acceptance criteria

The acceptance of the deliverables will be decided by the User Acceptance Team under the control of the Quality Director. The process and acceptance criteria are described in the Quality Management Plan summarized in § 8 of this document.

2.1.1.4 Not in the project scope

The following are not part of the project scope:

- ✓ Interface with the subsidiaries e-commerce applications
- ✓ Redesign of some subsidiaries' websites

2.1.1.5 Constraints

Below are the main constraints:

- ✓ The first subsidiary must be deployed at the latest March 2023, the last in March 2027, at the latest.
- ✓ The overall budget is 120 million euros over 4 years; the budget for the first year is 40 million euros and must not be exceeded.

2.1.1.6 Assumptions

- ✓ The shareholders renewed their support to the President of Globalinrance in order to continue the project.
- ✓ The employees of AssurTGE and its subsidiaries assigned to the project are available on time.

2.1.2 Work Breakdown Structure (WBS)

The works required to produce the deliverables are represented on the Work Breakdown Structure in annex 4.

The project is broken down into three successive releases followed by the specificities of each subsidiary. The content of the first release is defined in the functional specifications. The content of the following releases will be detailed gradually during the course of the project.

2.1.3 WBS Dictionary

The WBS dictionary in annex 5 describes the components of the WBS.

2.2 Schedule baseline

The table 2.4 below summarizes the milestones as defined to date. They will be revised at the beginning of each phase as described in § 6 Time Management Plan.

	Core System 1	Core System 2	Core System 3	Subsidiaries specificities
End of specifications	04/2021	-	-	-
End of design validation	08/2021	-	-	-
Start developments	09/2021	-	-	-
Start of acceptance tests	03/2022	-	-	-
Validation of the pilot (Start)	09/2022	-	-	-
Sart of generalization	03/2023	03/2024	03/2025	03/2027
Closing release	05/2023	05/2024	05/2025	05/2027

Table 2.4 Follow-up of milestones

2.3 Cost baseline

To determine the total cost of each release, the project manager will refer to the WBS (see annex 4) and proceed as below:

1. Estimate the costs of the components of the last level (level 5)
2. Estimate and calculate the costs of level 4 components
3. Estimate and calculate the costs of level 3 components
4. Sum the costs of level 3 components to get the cost of the release (excluding risks prevention costs)
5. Add the risks prevention costs to the cost calculated in step 4 to get the cost of release (excluding hardware and licenses)
6. Add the costs of equipment and licenses to the cost calculated in step 5 to get the release total budget.

The risks prevention cost is related to the activities required to mitigate the risks identified in the risk register.

Reserves will be made for a contingency plan. They will enable the sponsor to finance the "not identified" risks. They represent about 5 % of the total budget. They are not part of the costs baseline and will not be followed by the project manager.

	Core System 1	Core System 2	Core System 3	Subsidiaries specificities
	Budget in million euros (M€)			
Human resource				
Project management	2.8			
Specifications	2.8			
Design	4.2			
Development	14			
Acceptance & Tests	4.2			
Deployment	0.7			
Change management	0.7			
Closing	0.7			
Risk prevention	2.8			
Materials and licenses				
Servers & Other infrastructure	2.0			
Various licenses	1.0			
Sub-Total	36	26	25	33
Total	**120**			

Table 2.5. Budget baseline

The margin of uncertainty:

- ✓ Core System 1 = +/- 10 %
- ✓ Core System 2, Core System 3, Specific subsidiaries = +/- 50 %

The budgets of the Core System 2, Core System 3 and subsidiaries specificities are indicative and will be progressively refined during the course of the project.

Note that all requests for external resources (human, material and software) will be addressed to Procurement Department in accordance with AssurTGE's procurement process.

3 Change Management Plan

All change requests will follow the process below:

1. *Initiate the change request*: A change request can be initiated by the project manager, a stakeholder, or any member of the project team. The applicant completes the online change request form available in the project file at "Sharepoint / alphaproject / request-change /": a notification will be automatically sent to the project manager.
2. *Check the consistency of the request*: The project manager checks that the change request is consistent with the project charter. If the requested change is out of the scope defined in the project charter, the project manager will reject it.
3. *Validate the request*: If the request is consistent with the project charter, the project manager must pre-validate it and save it in the change request register: a notification will be automatically sent to the business managers who will have to validate it. This register should be kept up to date with the decisions and the rejection reasons (in case of rejection).
4. *Evaluate the change request*: If the request is validated by all managers, the project manager and the project team will assess the impact of the change request on the project scope, budget, schedule and quality.
5. *Propose options*: The project manager will propose options to respond to the change request.
6. *Approve or reject the request*: If the request does not change the project baselines, project management plan, project charter, or project processes, the project manager will approve it. Otherwise the project manager will submit the request to the Change Control Board (CCB) presenting the impacts and the options; the CCB will then decide whether to approve or reject the change.
7. *Inform the applicant*: The project manager will communicate the CCB's decision to the applicant.
8. *Update project references*: If the request is approved, the project manager will update the project baselines as well as the project management plan and all project documents impacted.

9. *Implement the requested change*: If the request is approved, the project team will implement the change according to the schedule.

4 Requirements Management Plan

4.1 Planning, monitoring and review of activities related to requirements

The project manager will have to document the stakeholder needs necessary to achieve the objectives of AlpaProject. For this purpose, he will conduct workshops to define and prioritize the functional and non-functional requirements. At the beginning of the session, he will remind the participants how to define them and the prioritization technique to follow.

He will maintain the prioritized requirement list up to date and integrate new business needs. To achieve this, at least once a month, he will organize a workshop dedicated to the review and re-prioritization of the requirements.

Requirements change requests will follow the procedure defined in § 3 Change Management Plan.

4.2 Structure of the traceability matrix

The requirements will be tracked with the traceability matrix shown in annex 7.

5 Scope Management Plan

5.1 Elaboration of the project scope

The project manager will have to organize workshops to develop the detailed description of Centragiciel and to define the required works to produce AlphaProject deliverables. The requirements document will be the input for each workshop. Participants will be chosen according to the business processes planned on the agenda. The group should be composed of business representatives, functional representatives, user representatives, technical representatives, and representatives of the integrator. Several workshops will be done in parallel if possible.

Below is the process to follow:

1. Prepare the workshop:
   - ✓ Select the group of business processes to discuss during the workshop (the agenda)
   - ✓ Create the group of participants based on the agenda
   - ✓ Plan the workshop
   - ✓ Three days (at the latest) before the date of the workshop, communicate to participants the document that covers the requirements related to the business processes in the agenda
2. Conduct the workshop
3. Formalize the output document "AlphaProject scope statement" for the business processes treated
   - ✓ Specify the part of scope statement covered by the workshop
   - ✓ Two days after the workshop, communicate to participants the document produced in the previous step
   - ✓ Collect participants feedbacks two days after the publication

- ✓ Finalize the document by considering the participants comments
- ✓ Distribute the final version of the document before the next session
- ✓ Validate the document at the next workshop

5.2 Construction of the Work Breakdown Structure (WBS)

In a workshop, the project team will break down the deliverables and the project work into components smaller and easier to monitor. The phases of the project life cycle will be used as the first level of decomposition (see example in Annex 4).

The inputs are the "Project Charter" and "AlphaProject scope statement".

At the end of the workshops, the project manager will publish the WBS and its dictionary to stakeholders.

The project team will check that the WBS covers all business processes expected and all project activities including those related to project management.

The WBS and its dictionary will then be validated at the next workshop (at the latest).

5.3 Formal acceptance of the deliverables

The deliverables acceptance will follow the procedure described below:

- ✓ The team installs the deliverable in the user acceptance environment (software deliverables) and communicates a delivery report to the "User Acceptance" manager.
- ✓ The User Acceptance team executes a test plan and raises bugs using the bug management tool.

- ✓ The User Acceptance manager communicates the test report to the Quality director, the project manager and the sponsor.
- ✓ If the deliverable meets the acceptance criteria, the acceptance manager will accept it. The project manager will organize an official meeting where the Quality director, the business representatives, the user representatives, the sponsor and the project manager decide the deployment.
- ✓ If the deliverable does not meet the acceptance criteria, the acceptance manager will detail the bugs that prevent accepting the deliverable and will raise the change requests for correction in accordance with the change request process.

5.4 Scope change request

The requests that change the scope will follow the process defined in the "Change Management Plan".

6 Time Management Plan

The duration of the works will be estimated in days. The workload of the smallest activity will not be lower than 0.25 day. Work performance will be measured once a month with Table 3.2 "Follow-up of performance" presented in Section 3.

The schedule will be developed progressively as described below:

For each work package:

1. Break down the work package of the WBS in activities.
2. Define dependencies between activities.
3. Put the activities in the execution order considering the dependencies.
4. Estimate the duration of activities, i.e. the number of periods of work required to complete each activity. The estimate must be done in the workshop by those who will work on the activities if possible, otherwise by their representatives.
5. Estimate the number of human resources (in man-days), hardware and software needed to carry out the activities.
6. Check and integrate the availability of resources (vacation for human resources, date of availability for hardware and software).
7. Create the schedule with the scheduling tool LogiProj using the schedule template available on SharePoint.
8. Compare the deliverable end date to the deadline constraint. Explore options to optimize the schedule if the date is beyond the deadline constraint and present them to the sponsor.
9. Have the schedule approved by the sponsor. Once approved, it becomes the baseline that will be used to monitor the project time.

Mandatory milestones are:

- ✓ The end of phase
- ✓ The delivery date of each deliverable

The Table 3.7 "Follow-up of milestones" in section 3 presents the timeline for "Core System 1". If there is a delay, the project manager will investigate the cause and recommend corrective actions for the next phase of the project.

The table below summarizes the role and responsibility of each actor involved in the process of development of the schedule.

Actor	Role and responsibility
Project Manager	✓ Coordinates and participates in project activities ✓ Creates schedule ✓ Proposes and presents options for optimization of the schedule to the sponsor ✓ Measures and presents once a month the performance of work in Steering Committee meetings
Project team member	✓ Assists the project manager to optimize the schedule ✓ Achieves the activities that are under his responsibility
Expert	Provides expertise
Sponsor	Approves the schedule

Table 2.6 role and responsibility of stakeholders

7 Cost Management Plan

See § 2.3 Cost Baseline for budget calculation.

In addition, the project manager will perform the actions below during the course of the project (for example at the end of each phase):

- ✓ Based on the risk register and the schedule, re-estimates the budget
- ✓ Confront the budget with the costs constraint, study the options to optimize the budget if it is beyond the constraint and present them to the sponsor.
- ✓ Have it approved by the sponsor.

Once the budget is approved, it becomes the new baseline that will be used to monitor the project cost.

The work performance will be measured once a month with the Table 3.2 – Follow-up of performance (see sections 3).

When a cost overrun is observed, the project manager will investigate the cause and propose corrective actions for the next phase of the project.

8 Quality Management Plan

As part of this project, the quality department must:

- ✓ Validate the deliverables
- ✓ Verify the compliance with the processes defined in this document
- ✓ Propose process improvements when necessary.

To validate the deliverables as part of system testing, the test manager must:

1. Prepare the validation
   - ✓ Define the strategy and the organization of the validation by specifying the scope and how to test the deliverables
   - ✓ Develop the test plan
   - ✓ Identify the required resources and check their availability
   - ✓ Estimate the workload and plan the required actions
   - ✓ Check that the test environments are operational and that deliverables can be tested
2. Validate the deliverables
   - ✓ Execute the test plan and raise bugs
   - ✓ Perform functional tests, tests of the interfaces between components, regression tests (especially between two versions) and performance tests
   - ✓ Analyze the test results and the quality of the deliverables
   - ✓ Verify if the conditions are met to install the deliverables in a User Acceptance Test environment for users
   - ✓ Deliver the test report

To check the compliance with the process, the validation manager must conduct a quality review at the end of each phase of the project. For this purpose, he must:

- ✓ Prepare and adapt a checklist of checkpoints according to the project phases.
- ✓ Evaluate the non-compliance detected and propose correction and improvement actions plan to the project manager when necessary
- ✓ Deliver a report of the review

All corrective, preventive, or improvement change requests must follow the change request process described in § 3 Change Management Plan.

The Table 2.7 below summarizes the quality indicators. They will be monitored monthly in the "quality review" meetings. Tables 3.4 and 3.5 in Section 3 measure the number of bugs detected and resolved in relation to the number of test cases performed.

Goal	Metric and expected limit
Compliance with the project management processes	Less than 5 % major "non-compliance" detected during the quality review
Quality of the deliverables	✓ 100 % test coverage ✓ No blocking bug, no major bug, less than 10 % of minor bugs

Table 2.7 Quality indicators expected

Types of bugs are defined as follows:

- ✓ A bug is a "Blocking" when it stops the validation (during testing).
- ✓ A bug is "major" when a feature ends with a false result; or a result that exceeds the tolerance threshold allowed by the requirement.
- ✓ The other types of bugs are considered "Minor".

9 Communication Management Plan

Table 3.2 in section 3 will be used to monitor and control the project performance. For the communication purpose, the project manager will extract useful information.

Table 2.8 below presents a template of the simplified progress report (See comments on the columns in section 3).

	Values			Variances		Performance Indexes		
WBS Element	Planned Value (PV)	Earned Valeur (EV)	Actual Cost (AC)	Cost Variance (CV = EV-AC)	Schedule Variance (CV = PV-AC)	Cost Performance Index (CPI = EV/AC)	Schedule Performance Index (SPI = EV/PV)	Cost re-estimated
Project management								
Specifications								
Design								
Developments								
Testing								
Deployment								
Change management								
Risk prevention								
Release Closing								

Table 2.8. Template of the progress report

In addition to the simplified progress report, the project manager will present the details below:

- ✓ Performance analysis
- ✓ Work completed during the period
- ✓ Work to do in the following period
- ✓ The current state of risk and major problems
- ✓ The summary of changes approved during the period
- ✓ Other relevant points

The Stakeholder register is available on "SharePoint" in the project folder. It will need to be completed and updated throughout the project life cycle.

For all meetings, the organizer must send the agenda and the documents required for preparation to the participants, at the latest, 3 days before the meeting. By default, recurring meetings with subsidiaries will be done in videoconference rooms. In this case, the organizer must ensure that videoconference rooms are available and operational. All participants must read the documents published before the meeting and prepare questions and proposals. Meetings must start and finish on time. During the meeting, mobile phones must be put in "silence" mode. After each meeting, the organizer must publish the meeting minutes the following day at the latest.

The table below summarizes the types of formal communication planned. For all informal exchanges, stakeholders must contact the project manager to decide what to do.

Type of communication	Description	Frequency	Participants	Maximum duration	Organizer
Simplified progress report with comments	Table of the performance indicators, risk status	Weekly	Publication on the SharePoint followed by automatic notification to all stakeholders	NA	Project Manager
Group members meeting	Sharing of activities and problems between team members	Every day	Group leaders, group members	15 min	Group leaders
Project team meeting	Detailed progress report and risk analysis	Weekly	Group leaders, Business representatives	60 min	Project Manager
Risks review - Status of the preventive actions	Monitoring the progress of preventive actions for risk - Identification of new risks	Weekly	Group leaders, group members, Business representatives	60 min	Project Manager
Product demonstration	Demonstration of the features implemented	Every 2 months	Project team-all stakeholders	45 min	Project Manager
AssurTGE Steering Committee	Presentation of the progress of the project, risk status -Decision making	Monthly	Business, representatives sponsor	60 min	Project Manager
Steering committee extended to the subsidiaries	Presentation of the project status, risk status, next steps of the project	Every 2 months	Sponsor, Subsidiaries directors	60 min	Project Manager

Table 2.9. Communication types planned

10 Risk Management Plan

A risk is an uncertain event or condition that, if it occurs, has a positive or negative effect on one or more project objectives such as scope, schedule, cost and quality.

The project manager and his team will follow the process defined in this paragraph to manage AlfaProject's risks.

10.1 Methodology

The steps to follow are described below:

Step 1: Identify the risks

For each workpackage of the WBS, the project manager will determine the risks for each of the categories listed in the § 10.5. He will complete his research by analyzing the assumptions and constraints using the table 2.10 below, questioning experts and consulting the list of risks encountered in previous projects. The final list must be approved in a risk review session before moving to the next step.

Hypothesis or constraints	Could this hypothesis or constraint be false? (Yes/No)	If the hypothesis or the constraint is false, would this impact the project? (Yes/No)	Does it lead to a risk?

Table 2.10. Example: assumptions and constraints analysis.

When a hypothesis or a constraint leads to risk, describe the risk according to the template: "statement of the assumption/constraint" can reveal false and leads to "statement of the consequence on the objective of the project".

At the end of this step, the following fields of the risk register might have been filled:

- ✓ Title
- ✓ Description
- ✓ Causes (if already known)
- ✓ Responses (if already known)
- ✓ Planned date of the response (if already known)

Step 2: Analyze the risks

The project manager will follow the actions below to analyze the risks identified in the previous step:

- ✓ For each risk, determine the likelihood and impact according to scales defined in the tables 2.11 and 2.12 below.
- ✓ Determine the severity: unacceptable, critical, significant and Not significant by referring to the table 2.13
- ✓ Decide the risks that need a response

The probability is measured on a scale of 4 levels:

Level	Probability	
4	90 - 99 %	Near certainty
3	50 - 89 %	More likely
2	10 - 49 %	Less likely
1	1 - 9 %	Not likely

Table 2.11. Probability definition

The impact (case of threat) is measured on a scale of 5 levels as defined in the table 2.12 below: Very low, Low, Moderate, High and Very high.

Project objectives	Scales of impact				
	Very Low	**Low**	**Moderate**	**High**	**Very High**
Cost	Overcost < 5 %	Overcost 5 % - 10 %	Overcost 10 % - 20 %	Overcost 20 % -40 %	Overcost > 40 %
Time	Delay < 5 %	Delay 5 % - 10 %	Delay 10 % - 20 %	Delay 20 % - 40 %	Delay > 40 %
Scope	Custom labels are missing but standard labels are displayed	Labels and texts remain understandable by the user	Functional content impacted but the result remains coherent (Excluding wording and texts)	Functional content impacted and the result is inconsistent	The module is unusable
Quality	Only 2 labels are impacted by the use case	More than 2 labels are impacted by the use case	The result does not match the specified functional rules	Incoherent result is displayed	The module is unusable

Table 2.12. Definition of Impact Scales (case of threat)

Impact / Probability	Very High	High	Moderate	Low	Very Low
Near Certainty	Unacceptable	Unacceptable	Critical	Significant	Significant
More Likely	Unacceptable	Critical	Significant	Not significant	Not significant
Less Likely	Unacceptable	Critical	Significant	Not significant	Not significant
Not Likely	Critical	Significant	Not significant	Not significant	Not significant

Table 2.13 Definition of risk severity

Step 3: Plan risk responses

The project manager will create a working group composed of members of the project team and any other stakeholder that can bring its expertise to find a solution to the risks. To prepare the workshops, he will assign the risk to participants based on their competence and expertise. They will do the actions listed below:

For each of the risks decided in the previous step,

- ✓ Study the responses proposed in step 1 and deepen them
- ✓ Define options if necessary
- ✓ Choose an option (contingency plan)
- ✓ Determine the secondary risks (risks caused by the implementation of the response)
- ✓ Determine residual risks (risks remained after the implementation of the response)
- ✓ Define the actions to take in case the contingency plan turns out to be inadequate (fallback plan)
- ✓ Describe the triggers which will help to know when to start the execution of the contingency plan
- ✓ Assign an owner for the risk: the owner will have the responsibility to monitor the triggers and give the "go" for the execution of the action plan when the conditions are met. He is responsible for the implementation of the response plan.
- ✓ Define the budget and the schedule of the activities related to the responses.

If the risk response plan changes at least one objective of the project, the change must be approved in accordance with the change management plan process described in § 3 Change Management Plan.

Participants can refer to the response's strategies below:

Thread:

- ✓ Avoid the risk by defining actions to eliminate it entirely. It can be for example: remove the part of the project or the resource likely to cause the risk, extend the time, reduce the scope, etc.
- ✓ Transfer the impact and the responsibility of the response to a third party (as we do when we buy insurance).
- ✓ Mitigate it by lowering its probability or impact to an acceptable threshold or both. For example, by performing more tests, or validating a concept with a prototype, etc.
- ✓ Simply accept the risk by not taking any action until it occurs. Define a contingency plan to apply in case the risk occurs.

Opportunity:

- ✓ Exploit the opportunity by removing the cause of its uncertainty. For example: add resources or reorganize the project outright.
- ✓ Share with a third party the impact and the responsibility of the response. For example, develop a partnership with a specialized third party that will achieve our work.
- ✓ Enhance the opportunity by increasing its probability or impact or both. For example, assigning a more experienced resource to an activity to complete it before the planned end date.
- ✓ And as for a threat, simply accept the opportunity by not taking any action until the event occurs.

Step 4: Monitor and control the risks: Assess the result of the action plan execution

The project manager should ensure the application of the actions below during the project lifecycle:

- ✓ Monitor the risk triggers
- ✓ Implement the action plans and control their application
- ✓ Reassess the risks
- ✓ Identify new risks and manage them by following the process described in this paragraph
- ✓ Communicate on risks, example: number of risks occurred last month, Effectiveness of the responses, status of current risk responses, number of risks that will potentially occur the next month and the provisions planned to manage them.
- ✓ Improve the risk management process when necessary
- ✓ Compare remaining risk budget to the project risks and check if they are sufficient to cover all the project risks.

10.2 Roles and responsibilities (in risk management process)

All stakeholders are likely to participate in the risk management process, including those outside the project team. The table below provides only the main actors.

Roles	Responsibilities
Project Manager	✓ Manages all the stages of the risk management process ✓ Develops the risk response plan ✓ Presents the response plan to steering committee members ✓ Updates the project management plan, the risk register and any other documents related to the risk management process.
Project Committee	Participates in all stages of the risk management process.
Steering Committee	✓ Approves the risk response plans when required ✓ Allocates the resources required for the implementation of the response plans.

Table 2.14. Roles and responsibilities

10.3 Budget (extract of calculation example)

Risk description	Consequence	Probability	Calculation of provisions (Time)	Calculation of provisions (Cost)
Delay in receiving the AXM software license that could postpone the start of the management module integration leading to deliver Centragiciel v1 late.	✓ Cost: increase of 150 k€ ✓ Time: 2 weeks delay (10 days)	40 %	10 days x 40 % = 4 days	150 k€ x 40 % = > + 60 k€ (Increase)
Renegotiation of pricing conditions with our provider People2YourC that could lower the current daily rate and reduce the team cost.	Cost: decrease of 20 k€	60 %		20 k€ x 60 % => -12 k€ (Decrease)
The internal IT department will probably move many workstations this year; which will slow down developments if this is done	✓ Cost: increase of 200 k€ ✓ Time: a week delay (5 days)	20 %	5 days x 20 % = 1 day	200 k€ x 20 % => + 40 k€ (Increase)
Total Provisions			**5 days (4 + 1)**	**+ 88 k€ (+ 60-12 + 40)**

Table 2.15. Example: Cost of risk calculation

10.4 Risk review schedule

The risk review will be done every week (see § 9 communication plan). In addition to this frequency, when necessary, the project manager can schedule a specific workshop to review the risks.

10.5 Risk categories

The initial list of categories below will help to explore the sources of risk. It must be updated throughout the project lifecycle:

- ✓ Definition of needs
- ✓ Quality
- ✓ Resources
- ✓ Time
- ✓ Technology
- ✓ Application of the project management plan recommendations
- ✓ Assumptions
- ✓ Dependency
- ✓ Sponsor and stakeholders Involvement

Annex 7 - Requirements traceability matrix (extract)

ID	Type (functional, performance, etc.)	Description	Reference Specs (*)	Reference Use Case (*)	Reference Test case (*)	Status (Done/ In progress)	Comment
EXG001	Functional	The software must be able to authenticate a member using his membership card.	I.11	CU2	CT2	Done	
EXG002	Functional	The system must automatically route the call to an experienced agent when the caller's case involves litigation or the person is identified as a VIP.	II.1.1.1	CU24	CT24	In progress	The criteria that define the "experienced agent" must be listed with the functional manager.
EXG003	Functional	The software must automatically display a form to create the caller's record when he is not identified in the database.	II.1.1.2	CU25	CT25	Done	
EXG004	Functional	The software must automatically record in its database, information from the various channels used by customers to contact agencies: email, internet, mobile internet, telephone, fax, SMS.					
EXG005	Functional	The software must provide the possibility to extend the list of the channels mentioned in EXG004.					

(*) References are to the specific documents dedicated respectively to the specifications, use cases and test cases.

ID	Type (functional, performance, etc.)	Description	Reference Specs (*)	Reference Use Case (*)	Reference Test case (*)	Status (Done/ In progress)	Comment
EXG006	Functional	The software must provide input help; for example, to propose the names of cities or towns that are attached to a postal code.					Provide the data to propose.
EXG007	Functional	The software must automatically pre-fill the caller's known data when it is identified.					
EXG008	Functional	The software must automatically display a member's record when the caller is identified.					
EXG009	Functional	The software must record the date and author of changes made on data.					
EXG010	Functional	The software must have indicators that measure a member's use of his personal space: the number of connections in the year, date of last connection, list of modules consulted and their number of consultations.					

(*) References are to the specific documents dedicated respectively to the specifications, use cases and test cases.

ID	Type (functional, performance, etc.)	Description	Reference Specs (*)	Reference Use Case (*)	Reference Test case (*)	Status (Done/ In progress)	Comment
EXG011	Functional	The software must record member's indicators of satisfaction based on the results of satisfaction surveys that are done once every 2 months.					
...	...	...					
EXG650	Performance	The software must have a response time of less than 2 seconds at startup and about millisecond during navigation.					
EXG651	Performance	The software must be able to serve 150,000 users simultaneously from 6:00 am to 12:00 pm local time and 100,000 from 12:00 pm to 10:00 pm					
EXG652	Availability	The software must be available between 6:00 am and 10:00 pm local in each country in which it's used.					
EXG653	Scalability	The software must be able to manage 500,000 users during the first 6 months after the start of production, and 800,000 users later.					

(*) References are to the specific documents dedicated respectively to the specifications, use cases and test cases.

ID	Type (functional, performance, etc.)	Description	Reference Specs (*)	Reference Use Case (*)	Reference Test case (*)	Status (Done/ In progress)	Comment
EXG654	Robustness	The software should continue to work properly in offline mode if the connection to the central server is down.					
EXG655	Ergonomics	The interfaces must comply with each subsidiary's graphic charter.					
EXG656	Ergonomics	Centragiciel must provide fast access links from the home page to the four main features common to the subsidiaries.					
EXG657	Simplicity	The software package should be easy to use for users who have completed 4 hours of training.					
…	…	…					

(*) References are to the specific documents dedicated respectively to the specifications, use cases and test cases.

Table 2.16. requirements traceability matrix

Section 3: Tracking tools

Critical dependencies

Follow-up of performance

Follow-up of resources

Follow-up of bugs compared to test cases (cumulation)

Follow-up of bugs (per month)

Risk monitoring

Follow-up of milestones

Follow-up of the critical dependencies

Deliverable expected	Release Manager	Planned delivery date	Revised delivery date	Validator	Acceptance criteria
Leaves calculation engine	Editor RX	mm/dd/yyyy	mm/dd/yyyy	F.A	The output data of the execution of the four main functions are compliant with the specifications.
Summary of the interfaces with legacy applications	Essin D	mm/dd/yyyy	mm/dd/yyyy	D.A.	Review and approved by the architecture team.
Etc.					

Table 3.1. Critical dependencies

Follow-up of performance

	Values			Variances		Performance Indexes		
Date of follow-up	**Planned Value (PV)**	**Earned Valeur (EV)**	**Actual Cost (AC)**	**Cost Variance (CV = EV-AC)**	**Schedule Variance (CV = PV-AC)**	**Cost Performance Index (CPI = EV/AC)**	**Schedule Performance Index (SPI = EV/PV)**	**Cost re-estimated**
mm/dd/yyyy								
mm+1/dd/yyyy								
mm+2/dd/yyyy								
mm+3/dd/yyyy								
mm+4/dd/yyyy								
mm+5/dd/yyyy								
Etc.								
mm+N/dd/yyyy								

Table 3.2. Follow-up of performance

<u>Note</u>:

Preparation of the follow-up:

- Date of follow-up: fill in the column "Date of follow-up" according to the duration of the "release"
- Planned Value (Budgeted Cost for Work Scheduled): for each date, sum the planned costs of the *tasks that must have been performed at the follow-up date*. When only part of a task is scheduled to be performed on the follow-up date, count only the cost of that part (and not that of the entire task).

During the course of the project:

At the current follow-up date,

- Actual Cost (Actual Cost of Work Performed): calculate the sum of the *effort really spent on each task* since the beginning of the project.
- Earned value (Budgeted Cost for Work Performed):
    - Calculate the planned costs of each *task completed* since the beginning of the project. This is the percentage of the task completed multiplied by the total planned cost of the task.
    - Sum those calculated costs of all tasks performed.
- Cost re-estimated: based on the estimate of the remaining tasks, recalculate the new cost value for each "Date of follow-up".

Analysis:

- Schedule Performance Index (SPI): when its value is less than 1, it means that the amount of work performed is less than scheduled: the project is behind the forecast. A value greater than 1 means that the amount of work done is higher than expected: the project is ahead of the forecast.
  Example: An SPI of 0.8 indicates a delay of 20 % from the planned end date. An SPI of 1.2 indicates an advance of 20 % from the planned end date.
- Cost Performance Index (CPI): when its value is less than 1, this indicates a cost overrun. A value greater than 1

indicates that the actual cost of the work performed is less than the planned cost of the same work at the date of the follow-up.
Example: A CPI of 0.8 indicates that the cost of the work performed is 20 % higher than the budget planned for this same work (cost overrun of 20 % compared to the planned budget). A CPI of 1.2 indicates that the cost of the work done is less than 20 % compared to the budget planned for this same work.

Note that the calculations requested above are achievable with the planning tool.

Follow-up of resources

Values in the table below are given as an example.

Date	Number of resources planned	Actual number of resources	Forecasts
mm/dd/yyyy	20	16	
mm+1/dd/yyyy	25	18	
mm+2/dd/yyyy	25	20	
mm+3/dd/yyyy	25	25	
mm+4/dd/yyyy	30	28	30
mm+5/dd/yyyy	35		37
mm+6/dd/yyyy	35		37
mm+7/dd/yyyy	35		37
mm+8/dd/yyyy	35		37
mm+9/dd/yyyy	35		37
mm+10/dd/yyyy	35		37
mm+11/dd/yyyy	35		37
mm+12/dd/yyyy	35		37
Etc.			

Table 3.3. Follow-up of resources

Follow-up of bugs compared to test cases (cumulation)

	Tests (cumulation)			Bugs (cumulation)			
Date	**Planned test cases**	**Test cases executed once**	**Successful test cases**	**Unresolved critical bugs**	**Resolved critical bugs**	**Other bugs unresolved**	**Other bugs resolved**
mm/dd/yyyy							
mm+1/dd/yyyy							
mm+2/dd/yyyy							
mm+3/dd/yyyy							
mm+4/dd/yyyy							
mm+5/dd/yyyy							
mm+6/dd/yyyy							
mm+7/dd/yyyy							
mm+8/dd/yyyy							
mm+9/dd/yyyy							
mm+10/dd/yyyy							
mm+11/dd/yyyy							
mm+12/dd/yyyy							
Etc.							

Table 3.4. Follow-up of bugs compared to the tests-case (cumulation)

Follow-up bugs (per month)

	Identification				Qualification				Follow-up	Treatment		
NO.	**Risk**	**Consequence**	**Cost of risk**	**Date of identification**	**Probability**	**Forecast date when the risk could occur**	**Impact level**	**Severity**	**Status**	**Risk response action plan**	**Owner of the risk**	**Action date**
1												
2												
3												
4												
5												
6												
7												
8												
9												
10												
11												
12												
13												

Table 3.5. Follow-up bugs (per month)

Follow-up of risk

	Identification				Qualification				Follow-up	Treatment		
NO.	**Risk**	**Consequence**	**Cost of risk**	**Date of identification**	**Probability**	**Forecast date when the risk could occur**	**Impact level**	**Severity**	**Status**	**Risk response action plan**	**Owner of the risk**	**Action date**
1												
2												
3												
4												
5												
6												
7												
8												
9												
10												
11												
12												
13												

Table 3.6. Risks monitoring

Follow-up of milestones

Provide regularly on each monitoring date an update of the milestone.

	J0	J1	J2	J3	J4	J5	J6
Follow-up date	End specifications	End design validation	Start developments	Start of User Acceptance	Pilot validation site	Start of generalization	Release closing
mm/dd/yyyy	mm/dd/yyyy	mm+2/dd/yyyy	mm+2/dd/yyyy	mm+6/dd/yyyy	mm+8/dd/yyyy	mm+9/dd/yyyy	mm+10/dd/yyyy
mm+1/dd/yyyy							
mm+2/dd/yyyy							
mm+3/dd/yyyy							
mm+4/dd/yyyy							
mm+5/dd/yyyy							
mm+6/dd/yyyy							
mm+7/dd/yyyy							
mm+8/dd/yyyy							
mm+9/dd/yyyy							
mm+10/dd/yyyy							
mm+11/dd/yyyy							
mm+12/dd/yyyy							
Etc.							

Table 3.7. Follow-up of milestones

Acknowledgements

First and foremost, I want to acknowledge Margaret Kennedy who introduced me to her sister Geraldine Muldoon.

I Would like to express my special thanks of gratitude to Geraldine Muldoon, who kindly read much of the manuscript and provided valuable inputs.

Bibliography and Internet References

Projects

- ✓ A Guide to the Project Management Body of Knowledge (PMBOK Guide) Fifth Edition
- ✓ Rita Mulcahy's PMP Exam Prep, Seventh Edition
- ✓ Mike Griffiths, PMI - ACP Exam Pep Second Edition

Anecdotes

- ✓ http://www.sciencesetavenir.fr/Espace/astrophysique/ondes-gravitationnelles-comment-la-collision-de-2-trous-noirs-fait-vibrer-l-univers_23389
- ✓ http://dailygeekshow.com/Mythologie-grece-anecdotes/
- ✓ http://www.pheniciens.com/articles/Decouverte.php

www.ingramcontent.com/pod-product-compliance
Lightning Source LLC
Chambersburg PA
CBHW030620220526
45463CB00004B/1360
9781791888602